A QUICK COURSE IN

EXCEL

For Windows

JOYCE COX

PATRICK KERVRAN

PUBLISHED BY
Online Press Incorporated
14320 NE 21st Street, Suite 18
Bellevue, WA 98007
(206) 641-3434

Publisher's Cataloging in Publication
(prepared by Quality Books Inc.)

Cox, Joyce, 1946–
     A quick course in Excel for Windows / Joyce Cox, Patrick Kervran.
  p. cm.
  Includes index.
  ISBN 1-879399-04-0

  1. Microsoft Windows (Computer programs). I. Kervran, Patrick, 1961– II. Title.

QA76.76.W56   005.4'3
                                     QBI91-168
                                           91-62153
                                             CIP

Printed and bound in the United States of America

1 2 3 4 5 6 7 8 9 H L O L 3 2 1 0

Distributed to bookstores by Publishers Group West, (800) 365-3453

Contents

Introduction

There are no two ways about it: Microsoft Excel 3.0 for Windows is a complex program. You can't roll worksheets, databases, charts, and macros into one sophisticated package and expect to maintain the simplicity of a single-purpose product. What's more, over the years Microsoft has added some impressive bells and whistles to Excel, culminating with the outlining, 3-D charting, and graphics capabilities of the latest version.

Sound daunting? Well, we have good news for Excel beginners: We've taken the mystery out of learning Excel. Because it's no secret that most software users take advantage of only about 20 percent of a program's features when performing routine tasks, in this book we get right to the heart of Excel. In no time at all, we have you creating worksheets you can put directly to use in your business. We don't think you should have to spend countless hours combing through hundreds of pages of Excel documentation or a 400-page book that details every last program feature, when all you need right now is a quick course in Excel's most often-used features.

If you spend a few minutes looking through *A Quick Course in Excel for Windows*, you'll see why we say that our books offer streamlined instruction. We don't give extraneous background information; we don't describe two or three ways to perform the same task; and we don't cover features you probably won't use (at least not right off the bat). Instead, we focus on how to use Excel to get your work done. We think people learn quicker and retain what they learn longer when they can see how to combine program features to generate end products that they can put to use immediately.

We start in Chapter 1 by creating a worksheet that records sales, and then we show you how to manipulate the information in the worksheet in various ways. In Chapters 2 and 3, we continue working with the worksheet from Chapter 1, gradually building experience with basic procedures and progressing to more advanced techniques. You should read these first three chapters in sequence, being careful to save your worksheets when we tell you to, so that you have what you need for future tasks.

You can read the last three chapters in any order, because each chapter focuses on a different topic and uses independent worksheets. In Chapter 4, we use a simple budget worksheet to explore outlining and charting. In Chapter 5, we build a worksheet for estimating project costs and create links to two other worksheets so that the totals account for indirect as well as direct costs. And in Chapter 6, we show how to define formatting styles and write macros to speed up the process of creating an invoice. We end the chapter by examining a macro that transfers information from the invoice to a sales log—creating a worksheet that is similar to the one we built in Chapters 1, 2, and 3.

In designing our worksheets, we have made each one general enough to be adapted easily to other business tasks, and in several chapters we suggest other situations in which the worksheets might apply. In this book, as in all *Quick Course* books, we have scattered handy tips and useful tidbits throughout each chapter so that when you have the time, you can look them over and learn even more about Excel. For those times when you need to refer back to a particular discussion or want to browse ahead, we use arrows and captions to draw your attention to key information and procedures so that you can easily spot them later on as you thumb through the book.

As we have said, learning Excel for Windows is by no means an easy task, but you don't have to tackle it all at once. Take a moment to see what we have in store for you. Then turn to Chapter 1, and let's get started.

1

Building a Simple Worksheet

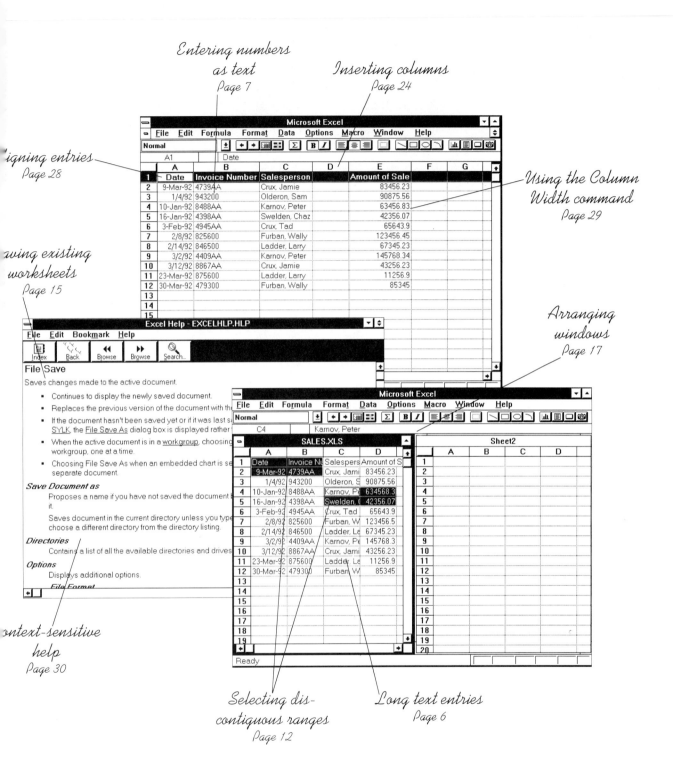

*Entering numbers
as text
Page 7*

*Inserting columns
Page 24*

*igning entries
Page 28*

*Using the Column
Width command
Page 29*

*ving existing
worksheets
Page 15*

*Arranging
windows
Page 17*

*ontext-sensitive
help
Page 30*

*Selecting dis-
contiguous ranges
Page 12*

*Long text entries
Page 6*

Y ou're probably sitting at your computer, anxious to start crunching numbers. But before we get going, we need to cover some basics, such as how to enter text and numbers, save files, move around a worksheet, edit and format entries, and print the results of your labors. After we discuss a few fundamentals, you'll easily be able to create the worksheets and charts we cover in the rest of the book.

We assume that you've already installed Windows 3 and Excel 3 on your computer. We also assume that you've worked with Windows before and that you know how to start programs, move windows, choose commands from menus, highlight text, and so on. If you are a Windows novice, we recommend that you take a look at *A Quick Course in Windows*, another book in the Quick Course series, which will help you quickly come up to speed.

To follow the instructions in this book, you must be using a mouse. Although it is theoretically possible to work in Windows and Excel using just the keyboard, we would not wish this fate on anyone, and most of our instructions involve using a mouse. Occasionally, however, when it is easier or faster to use the keyboard, we give the keyboard equivalent of the mouse action.

Well, let's get going. With the DOS prompt (C:>) on your screen, start Windows by typing *win* and pressing Enter. Then in Windows, start Excel by double-clicking the Microsoft Excel 3.0 icon in the Microsoft Excel 3.0 group window.

Starting Excel →

Getting Oriented

When you start Excel for the first time, your screen looks something like the one at the top of the facing page. At the top of the screen is the Microsoft Excel title bar, followed by the menu bar, from which you choose commands. Below the menu bar is the Toolbar, a new Excel feature that puts a host of often-used tools within easy reach. Below the Toolbar is the formula bar, in which you enter the values (text and numbers) and formulas that you'll use in your worksheet. At the left end of the formula bar, Excel displays an "address," called a cell reference, that tells you which part of the worksheet you are currently working with.

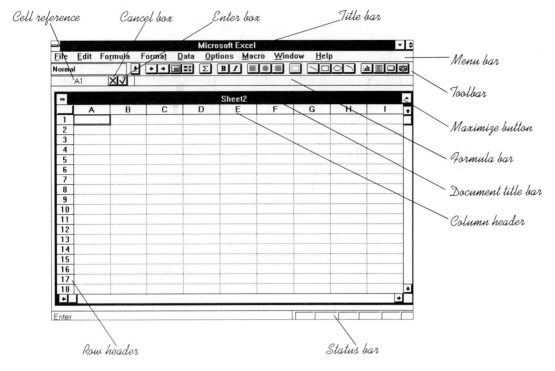

Cell reference   *Cancel box*   *Enter box*   *Title bar*

Menu bar

Toolbar

Maximize button

Formula bar

Document title bar

Column header

Row header   *Status bar*

Taking up the majority of the screen is the blank worksheet, which as you can see, is laid out in a grid of rows and columns like the ledger paper used by accountants. The rectangle at the junction of each column and row is called a cell. Each cell has a reference that consists of the letter displayed in the header at the top of the cell's column and the number displayed in the header at the left end of its row. For example, the reference of the cell in the top-left corner

Cell references

Excel group and icon

The Excel installation program creates the Microsoft Excel 3.0 group by default. If you do not have a Microsoft Excel 3.0 group, someone may have moved the Excel files to a different group. Open the other groups windows (Windows Applications is a likely candidate), locate the Microsoft Excel 3.0 icon, and double-click it to start the program. ♦

Other ways of starting

To start Excel (or any other Windows program) directly from the DOS prompt, type *win*, a space, and the name of the program. For Excel, type *win excel* and press Enter. Windows locates Excel, bypassing the Windows Program Manager. You can also start Excel with a document already loaded by typing *win excel*, a space, and the name of the document. ♦

Worksheet icons

You can also create icons for frequently used worksheets that will be displayed in Program Manager. Simply make a copy of the Microsoft Excel 3.0 icon, and then choose the Properties command from the File menu. Next, change the command line to include the name of the worksheet you wish to represent with an icon. ♦

of the worksheet, which is always active when you start Excel with a blank worksheet, is A1. The reference of the cell below A1 is A2, and the reference of the cell to the right of A1 is B1.

The worksheet has 256 columns, lettered A through IV, and 16,384 rows, numbered 1 through 16384, for a total of over 4 million cells. Potentially, you could create a worksheet 20 feet wide by 80 feet long—large enough for just about any set of calculations, short of the national budget.

At the bottom of the screen is the status bar, which displays useful information about menu and tool selections and about the status of keys, such as whether Num Lock or Caps Lock is turned on.

Entering Text

Most spreadsheets consist of blocks of text and numbers in table format on which you can perform various calculations. To make the tables easy to decipher, you usually give the columns and rows headings that describe their associated entries. Let's try entering a few headings now:

Entering headings →

1. With cell A1 selected on the blank worksheet, type *Date*. As you type, the text appears both in the formula bar and in the cell. In the formula bar, a blinking insertion point leads the way, telling you where the next character you type will be inserted. The Enter box

---

The status bar and Toolbar

If you don't see the status bar or the Toolbar, choose the Workspace command from the Options menu, select the Status Bar or Tool Bar option, and click OK. (For information about how to choose commands from menus, see page 13.) ♦

Mouse pointer shapes

The mouse pointer takes on different shapes depending on where it is on the screen. For example, the pointer is a cross when it is over the worksheet; an arrow when it is over a menu, the Toolbar, or a title bar; a double-headed arrow when it is over a row or column border; and a text tool (or I-beam) when it is over the formula bar. ♦

Selected cells

When you open an existing Excel worksheet, the cells that were selected when you closed the worksheet are still selected. ♦

and the Cancel box appear in the formula bar. Mean-
while, the indicator in the status bar changes from
Ready to *Enter*, because the text you have typed will
not be recorded in cell A1 until you "enter" it.

2. One way to record the entry is to click the Enter
    box—the box with a check mark in it to the left of the
    formula bar's entry area. Click the Enter box now.
    Excel records the Date heading in cell A1, and the
    indicator in the status bar changes back to *Ready*.
    Notice that the entry is left-aligned in its cell. Unless
    you tell Excel to do otherwise, it always left-aligns text
    entries and right-aligns numeric entries.

3. Click cell B1 to select it. The reference at the left end
    of the formula bar changes from A1 to B1, and the dark
    border that designates the active cell moves one cell to
    the right.

4. Type *Invoice Number*, but instead of clicking the Enter
    box to enter the heading in the cell, press the Tab key.
    Excel records the entry in cell B1 and moves the active
    cell to C1.

5. Type *Salesperson*, and press Tab.

6. Now enter one more heading. In cell D1, type *Amount
    of Sale*, and click the Enter box to record the entry.

Here's how the worksheet looks with the newly entered row
of headings:

*Recording entries
with the Enter box*

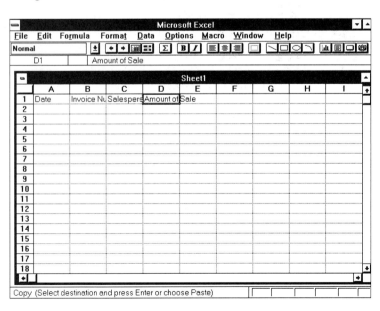

Long text entries →

Notice that the headings in cells B1, C1, and D1 are too long to fit in their cells. Until you entered the Salesperson heading in cell C1, the Invoice Number heading spilled over into C1, just as Amount of Sale now spills over from D1 into E1. After you entered the Salesperson heading, Excel truncated Invoice Number so that you could read the heading in C1. Similarly, after you entered Amount of Sale, Excel truncated Salesperson. The Invoice Number and Salesperson headings are still intact in B1 and C1, however. (If you're skeptical, click either cell and look at the formula bar.) In a minute, you'll learn how to adjust column widths to accommodate long entries.

That's it for the column headings. Now let's turn our attention to the rest of the table. We'll skip the Date and Invoice Number columns for the moment and enter the names of a few salespeople in last-name/first-name order in column C.

1. Click cell C2 to select it, and type *Crux, Jamie*.
2. Instead of clicking the Enter box, press the Enter key. Excel records the entry in cell C2 and makes cell C3 the active cell. (If the active cell doesn't move, see the tip below.)
3. Type *Olderon, Sam* in cell C3, and press Enter to record the entry and move to cell C4.
4. Next, type the following names in the Salesperson column, pressing Enter after each one:

Two Enter keys	Moving after pressing Enter	Alternate Navigation Keys
In Excel, the Enter key on the numeric keypad is functionally equivalent to the Enter key on the main keyboard. ♦	If the Enter key does not move the active cell down one row after recording an entry, choose the Workspace command from the Options menu, select the Move Selection After Enter option, and click OK. ♦	The Alternate Navigation Keys option in the Workspace dialog box provides additional keyboard shortcuts for worksheet navigation and formula entry. Many examples in this book will result in errors if this option is selected. For purposes of the examples provided here, leave this option deselected. ♦

C4	Karnov, Peter
C5	Swelden, Chaz
C6	Crux, Tad
C7	Furban, Wally
C8	Ladder, Larry
C9	Karnov, Peter
C10	Crux, Jamie
C11	Ladder, Larry
C12	Furban, Wally

Now let's enter the invoice numbers in column B. Usually, you will want Excel to treat invoice numbers—and social security numbers, part numbers, phone numbers, and other numbers that are used primarily for identification—as text rather than as numeric values on which you might want to perform calculations. If the "number" includes not only the digits 0 through 9 but also letters and other characters (such as hyphens), Excel recognizes it as text. However, if the number consists of only digits and you want Excel to treat it as text, you have to explicitly tell Excel to do so.

Entering numbers as text

For demonstration purposes, assume that your company has two regional offices, East and West. Both offices use invoice numbers with six characters. Invoices generated by the East office consist of four digits followed by AA, and those generated by the West office consist of six digits that end with 00. Follow these steps to see how Excel treats these invoice numbers:

1. Click cell B2 to select it, type *4739AA*, and press Enter. This invoice number consists of both digits and letters, so Excel treats the entry as text and left-aligns it.

2. In cell B3, which is now active, type *943200*, and press Enter. This invoice number consists of only digits, so Excel treats the entry as a numeric value and right-aligns it in its cell.

How do you tell Excel to also treat the entry that consists of only digits as text? You type the entry as a text string by enclosing it in double quotation marks, and you precede the entry with an equal sign to tell Excel that the value of the cell is equal to the text string. Follow the steps on the next page.

1. Hold down the Shift key and press the Enter key to move back up to cell B3.
2. Type =*"943200"*, and press Enter. This time, Excel treats the entry as text and left-aligns it in its cell.
3. Enter these invoice numbers in the indicated cells, being sure to enter those that end in 00 as text strings:

B4	8488AA
B5	4398AA
B6	4945AA
B7	825600
B8	846500
B9	4409AA
B10	8867AA
B11	875600
B12	479300

Your worksheet now looks like this:

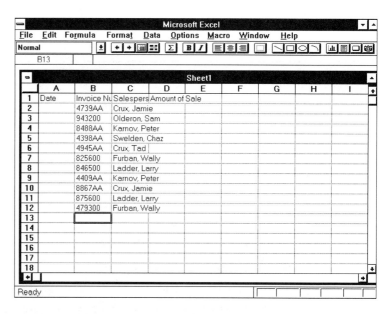

Entering Numeric Values

As you have seen, entering numeric values is just as easy as entering text. Follow along with the next few steps, as we enter the sales amounts in column D:

1. Click cell D2 to select the first cell in the Amount of Sale column, type *83456.23*, and press Enter. Excel records the entry and right-aligns it.
2. Enter the following amounts in the indicated cells, pressing Enter after each one:

D3	90875.56
D4	634568.30
D5	42356.07
D6	65643.90
D7	123456.45
D8	67345.23
D9	145768.34
D10	43256.23
D11	11256.90
D12	85345.00

Don't worry if Excel does not display these values exactly as you entered them (see the tip below). On page 50, we format these amounts so that they display as dollars and cents.

Entering Dates and Times

Even seasoned Excel users sometimes have difficulty entering dates and times in their worksheets. For dates and times to be displayed correctly, you must enter them "in format," which means that you must enter them in a format that Excel recognizes as a date or time. The following formats are recognized:

Entering in format

3/9/92	9:35 PM
9-Mar-91	9:35:43 PM
9-Mar	9:35
Mar-91	3-9-92 9:35

Long numeric values

As you have seen, Excel allows a long text entry to overflow into an adjacent empty cell and truncates the entry only if the adjacent cell also contains an entry. However, the program treats a long numeric value differently. If Excel displays # signs instead of the value you entered, the value is too large to display in the cell, and you must make the column wider to view it. Non-dollar values are displayed in scientific notation, and values with many decimal places are rounded off. For example, if you enter 12345678912345 in a standard-width cell (which is 8.43 characters in width), Excel displays 123E+13 (123 times 10 to the 13th power). If you enter 123456.789 in a standard-width cell, Excel displays 123456.8. In both cases, Excel leaves the underlying value unchanged, and you can widen the column to display the value in the format in which you entered it. (Adjusting the width of columns is discussed on page 28.) ◆

Let's get a feel for how Excel handles different date formats:

1. Enter the following dates in the indicated cells, pressing Enter after each one:

   A2   Mar 9, 1992
   A3   1/4/92
   A4   Jan 10, 92
   A5   January 16, 1992
   A6   February 3, 1992
   A7   2-8-92
   A8   2/14/92
   A9   3/2/92
   A10   3-12-92
   A11   23 Mar 1992
   A12   March 30, 1992

Excel might display the date differently from the way you entered it. Later, we'll come back and clean up the Date column so that the dates all appear in the same format.

As you can see below, you have now completed all the columns of this simple worksheet:

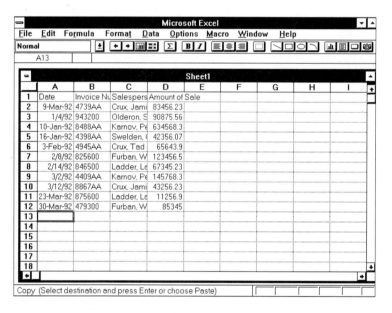

Selecting Ranges

Well, we've created a basic worksheet. But before we can show you some of the things you can do with it, we first need to discuss how to select blocks of cells, called ranges. Any rectangular block or blocks containing more than one cell is a range. A single column of cells is a range; a single row of cells is a range; and a block of cells ten columns wide and eight rows high is a range. Knowing how to select and work with ranges saves you time, because you can apply formats to or reference the whole range, instead of having to deal with its component cells individually.

Ranges have references that are composed of the address of the cell in the top-left corner of the rectangular block and the address of the cell in the bottom-right corner, separated by a colon. For example, the reference A1:B2 identifies the range that consists of cells A1, A2, B1, and B2.

Referring to ranges of cells

The simplest way to learn how to select ranges is to actually do it, so follow along as we demonstrate selecting ranges of different shapes and sizes.

1. Point to cell A1, hold down the mouse button, and drag diagonally to cell D12 without releasing the button. Notice that the reference at the left end of the formula bar reads *12R x 4C*, which indicates you are selecting a range of cells 12 rows high by 4 columns wide.

2. Release the mouse button. The range A1:D12 remains highlighted to indicate that it is selected. As shown below, cell A1—the cell where you started the selection—is white with a border to indicate that it is the active cell in the range.

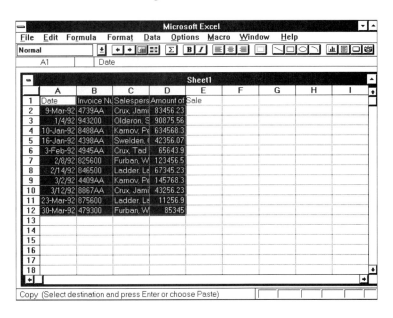

Selecting columns

3. Now move the mouse pointer to the header of column B, and click. Excel simultaneously deselects A1:D12 and selects all of column B—the range B1:B16384.

4. Now point to the header of column C, hold down the mouse button, and drag through the header for column D. Before you release the button, notice that the reference in the formula bar reads *2C*, indicating that two entire columns—the range C1:D16384—are selected.

Selecting rows

5. Move the pointer to the header of row 6, and click to select the entire row—the range A6:IV6.

Next, try selecting ranges with the keyboard:

Selecting with the keyboard

1. Select cell B6, hold down the Shift key, press the Right Arrow key twice and the Down Arrow key twice, and release the Shift key. The range B6:D8 is selected.

2. Select cell B6, hold down the Shift key, and press the Spacebar. Row 6—the range A6:IV6—is selected.

3. Select cell B6, hold down the Ctrl key, and then press the Spacebar. Column B—the range B1:B16384—is selected.

The ranges you just selected were all single blocks of cells, but ranges can be more than one block. Try this:

*Selecting dis-
contiguous ranges*

1. Use any method to select the range A1:B2.

2. Hold down the Ctrl key, and use the mouse to select the range C4:D5. Your worksheet now looks like this:

Moving within a range

When a range is selected, pressing the Enter and Tab keys moves the active cell within the range downward and to the right, respectively. Pressing the Enter and Tab keys while holding down the Shift key moves the active cell upward and to the left within the range. ♦

Automatic scrolling

When you drag beyond the window border to select a large range, Excel automatically scrolls new areas of the worksheet into view. ♦

Goto selection shortcut

A quick way to select a large range without using the mouse is to choose the Goto command from the Formula menu and enter the range reference in the Reference text box. When you click OK, Excel scrolls to the range and selects it. ♦

```
┌──────────────────────────────────────────────────────────────────────────┐
│ ▭                              Microsoft Excel                      ▼ ▲ │
├──────────────────────────────────────────────────────────────────────────┤
│ File  Edit  Formula  Format  Data  Options  Macro  Window  Help         │
├──────────────────────────────────────────────────────────────────────────┤
│ Normal        ▼  ◆ ◆ ▦ ▦  Σ  B I  ≣ ≣ ≣  ▭  ▢▢▢▢  ▥▣▢▩           │
├──────────────────────────────────────────────────────────────────────────┤
│    C4              │ Karnov, Peter                                        │
└──────────────────────────────────────────────────────────────────────────┘
```

	A	B	C	D	E	F	G	H	I
1	Date	Invoice Nu	Salespers	Amount of Sale					
2	9-Mar-92	4739AA	Crux, Jami	83456.23					
3	1/4/92	943200	Olderon, S	90875.56					
4	10-Jan-92	8488AA	Karnov, Pi	634568.3					
5	16-Jan-92	4398AA	Swelden, (	42356.07					
6	3-Feb-92	4945AA	Crux, Tad	65643.9					
7	2/8/92	825600	Furban, W	123456.5					
8	2/14/92	846500	Ladder, Le	67345.23					
9	3/2/92	4409AA	Karnov, Pe	145768.3					
10	3/12/92	8867AA	Crux, Jami	43256.23					
11	23-Mar-92	875600	Ladder, Le	11256.9					
12	30-Mar-92	479300	Furban, W	85345					
13									
14									
15									
16									
17									
18									

`Copy  (Select destination and press Enter or choose Paste)`

Notice that cell C4, the first cell of the second part of the range, is now the active cell, meaning that anything you type will appear in that cell.

Giving Excel Instructions

Now that you know how to select cells and ranges, let's quickly cover how you tell Excel what to do with your selection. You usually give Excel instructions by means of commands that are arranged in menus on the menu bar at the top of the window. Because this procedure is the same for all Windows applications, we assume that you are familiar with it and we provide only a quick review here. If you are a new Windows user, we suggest that you spend a little time becoming familiar with the mechanics of menus, commands, and dialog boxes before proceeding.

To choose a command from a menu, you first click the name of the menu in the menu bar. When the menu drops down, you simply click the name of the command you want. From the keyboard, you can press Alt or the forward slash key (/) to activate the menu bar, then press the underlined letter of the name of the menu, and finally, press the underlined letter of the command you want.

Choosing commands

Some command names are displayed in "gray" letters, indicating that you can't choose the commands. For example, the Paste command on the Edit menu appears in gray until you have used the Cut or Copy command.

Dialog boxes →

Some command names are followed by an ellipsis (...), indicating that you must supply more information before Excel can carry out the command. When you choose one of these commands, Excel displays a dialog box. You can then give the necessary information by typing in a text box or by selecting options from list boxes, drop-down list boxes, or groups of check boxes and option buttons. Clicking one of the command buttons—usually OK—closes the dialog box and carries out the command according to your specifications. Clicking Cancel closes the dialog box and also cancels the command. Other command buttons might be available to refine the original command or to open other dialog boxes with more options.

Keyboard Shortcuts

If you and your mouse don't get along and you prefer to use the keyboard, you can access many Excel commands by means of keyboard shortcuts. The list of shortcuts is extensive, and it would take a lot of space to reproduced it here. You can display the list by choosing the Keyboard command from the Help menu.

Saving Worksheets

With that brief overview out of the way, let's turn our attention back to the worksheet we have created and find out

File-naming conventions	Saving in another directory	File formats
DOS file-naming conventions apply to Excel worksheet names. The names you assign your worksheets must be eight characters or less and can include letters, numbers, and the following characters: _ ^ $! # % & - { } ( ). They cannot contain spaces, commas, or periods. ♦	By default, the worksheet will be saved in the directory in which you installed Excel. To save the worksheet in a different directory, simply select the directory you want from the Directories list in the Save As dialog box before clicking OK. ♦	By default, the worksheet will be saved in Normal format, which means it will be saved as an Excel 3 document. See page 68 for more information about how to change the file format. ♦

how to save it for future use. To save a brand new worksheet, you can choose either the Save or Save As command from the File menu. Excel displays a dialog box in which you specify the name of the worksheet. Follow these steps to save the worksheet now on your screen:

1. Choose Save from the File menu to display the Save As dialog box. In the Save Worksheet As text box, Excel suggests the name SHEET1.XLS.

2. Type *sales*. There's no need to supply an extension, because Excel will automatically use XLS to indicate that the file is an Excel spreadsheet.

3. Leave the other settings in the dialog box as they are for now, and click OK to carry out the command.

Saving new worksheets

When you return to the Excel window, notice that the name SALES.XLS has replaced Sheet1 in the worksheet's title bar.

From now on, you can choose Save from the File menu any time you want to save changes to this worksheet. Because Excel already knows the name of the worksheet, it simply saves the worksheet without displaying a dialog box, by overwriting the previous version with the new version.

Saving existing worksheets

If you want to save the changes you have made to a worksheet but preserve the previous version, you can assign the new version a different name by choosing the Save As command from the File menu, entering the new name in the Save Worksheet As text box, and clicking OK.

Preserving previous version

Save options

When you click the Options button in the Save As dialog box, Excel offers several options. Selecting the Create Backup File option causes Excel to create a copy of the previously saved version of the worksheet before overwriting it with the new version. Excel gives the backup copy the extension BAK. Selecting this option thus allows you to return to a previous version of a worksheet.

You can also assign a password of up to 15 characters in the Protection Password text box. Then Excel will require that the password be entered correctly before it will open the worksheet. The Write Reservation Password option works the same way, except that Excel will open a read-only version of the worksheet without requiring the password. The read-only version can be altered but can be saved only with a different name. Selecting the Read-Only Recommended option warns users that the worksheet should be opened as read-only. Excel does not, however, prevent users from opening the worksheet in the regular way. ♦

Creating New Worksheets

Having saved our worksheet, let's create a new one so that
we can see how to work with more than one document.
Follow these steps:

1. Choose the New command from the File menu.

2. Click OK to create a new worksheet. (We talk more
    about creating new charts on page 103 and about
    creating new macro sheets on page 145.) Excel opens
    a new blank worksheet with the name Sheet2, overlap-
    ping SALES.XLS. Your screen looks like this:

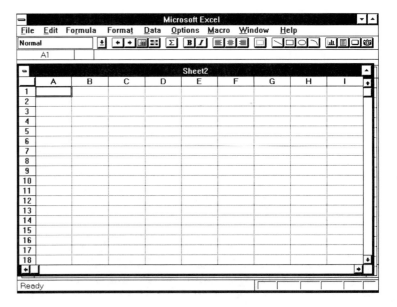

That's all there is to it. You now have two worksheets open
on your screen with which to experiment.

Manipulating Windows

Let's take a moment to review some window basics. Being
able to work with more than one worksheet open at a time is
useful, especially if you frequently need to use the same set
of numbers in different worksheets. For example, you might
use the same raw data to develop a budget or work out a trial
balance or create an income statement. Follow these steps to
see how easy it is to move from one worksheet to another:

1. Click any visible part of SALES.XLS to make it the active worksheet. If you can't see any of SALES.XLS, choose it from the list of open documents at the bottom of the Window menu. Notice that the color of its title bar changes to indicate that it is the active worksheet.

2. Choose Arrange All from the Window menu. Excel arranges the two worksheets so that they each occupy half the screen, like this:

Arranging windows

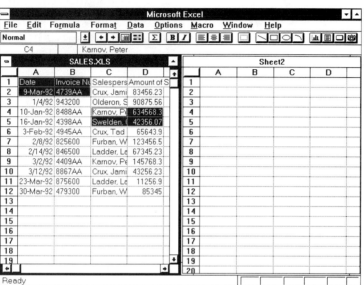

3. Click anywhere in Sheet2 to make it the active worksheet. Notice that scroll bars appear only in the active window. Any entries you make and any commands you choose will now affect only this worksheet.

4. Click the Maximize button (the up arrowhead in the top-right corner of the window). Sheet2 expands to fill the screen, completely obscuring SALES.XLS.

Maximizing windows

5. Pull down the Window menu again. Notice that the names of the two open worksheets appear at the bottom of the menu. A check mark indicates the active one.

6. Choose SALES.XLS from the Window menu. The two worksheets switch places, and SALES.XLS now completely obscures Sheet2.

These simple techniques work equally well whether you have two worksheets open or ten. (You can have as many as 24 files open at one time, but we've found that four is the practical limit if you want to be able to see them all and do useful work.)

Moving Around

The fastest way to move around the worksheet is with the mouse. As you've seen, clicking any cell activates that cell and puts its reference in the left end of the formula bar. To display parts of the worksheet that are currently out of sight, you can use the scroll bars, which function the same way as scroll bars in all Windows applications.

Using the scroll bars to bring cells into view does not change the active cell. As a result, you can pause in the middle of making an entry to view a cell in a different area of the worksheet and then return to the active cell with your incomplete entry still in the formula bar, just as you left it. Try this:

1. Select cell A1 in SALES.XLS to make it active.

2. Using the arrows at the bottom of the right scroll bar and the right end of the bottom scroll bar, bring cell P37 into view.

Displaying the active cell

3. Choose Show Active Cell from the Formula menu. Excel scrolls the worksheet to bring cell A1, the active cell, back into view.

As you know, you can also use the keyboard to move around the worksheet. The keys you'll use most often are the Tab and Enter keys, but as you gain more experience with Excel you might find other keys useful. Here's a list of navigation keys and what they do:

Scroll bars

The right scroll bar moves the worksheet up and down, and the bottom scroll bar moves the worksheet left and right. To move quickly to other parts of the worksheet, hold down the Shift key and drag the scroll boxes. The row and column references in the formula bar will change rapidly. Release the mouse button when the reference reaches the row or column you want to view. Drag the scroll boxes to the ends of the scroll bars to display cell IV16384.

No matter where you scroll to in a worksheet, the minute you begin typing, you return instantly to the active cell. ♦

Relocating the active cell

Using the keyboard to navigate a worksheet always relocates the active cell. To view another area of the worksheet without changing the active cell, simply use the scroll bars. ♦

Enter	Moves active cell down one cell.
Shift-Enter	Moves active cell up one cell.
Tab	Moves active cell right one cell.
Shift-Tab	Moves active cell left one cell.
PageUp	Moves screen down one screenful and activates a cell in screen's top row.
PageDown	Moves screen down one screenful and activates a cell in screen's top row.
Home	Moves active cell to column A in current row.
Ctrl-Home	Moves active cell to cell A1.
End	Moves active cell to last column that has entries in current row.
Ctrl-End	Moves active cell to last cell in document.

Moving the active cell

Another way to move around the worksheet is with the Goto command. Try this:

1. Choose Goto from the Formula menu to display this dialog box:

Jumping to a specific cell

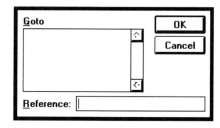

2. Type the reference of the cell that you want to go to. For this example, type *Z46* in the Reference text box, and click OK. Immediately, Excel scrolls the worksheet so that column Z and row 46 are visible.

3. Press Ctrl-Home to return to the top-left corner of the worksheet.

Editing Basics

In this section, we briefly cover some simple ways of revising and manipulating worksheets so that in subsequent chapters we can give general editing instructions without having to go into great detail.

Changing Entries

First, let's see how to change individual entries. Glancing at the Amount of Sale column in SALES.XLS, notice that the amount in cell D4 is suspiciously large compared with all the other amounts. Suppose that you check this number and find to your disappointment that the amount should be 63456.83, not 634568.3. Here's how you correct the number without having to retype the whole thing:

1. Select cell D4.
2. Move the pointer to the formula bar between the 6 and the 8, and click. Excel creates a blinking insertion point between the two numbers.
3. Type a period (.).
4. Click between the second period and the 3, and press Backspace to delete the second period.
5. Press Enter to record the corrected entry in the cell.

Copying Entries

You can copy any entry or group of entries anywhere within the same worksheet or to a different worksheet. Copy operations involve the use of two commands: Copy and Paste (or Insert Paste). Follow these steps:

1. Select A1:D12, and choose Copy from the Edit menu. A dotted rectangle, called a marquee, surrounds the selection, like this:

The Clipboard	**Temporary storage**	**Clipboard contents**
The Windows Clipboard is a temporary storage place used to hold cut or copied data from all Windows applications. It can also be used to transfer data from the documents of one application to those of another. ♦	Because the Windows Clipboard is a temporary storage space, exiting Windows or turning off your computer erases any information that is stored there, unless you save the Clipboard file. See the Windows documentation for more information. ♦	If you cut or copy cells and double-click the Clipboard icon in Program Manager, instead of displaying a copy of the cells and their contents, the Clipboard indicates the cut or copied range size. For example, *Copy 3R x 3C* indicates a range three rows high by three columns wide. This display has no effect on the result of pasting the cut or copied cells, however. ♦

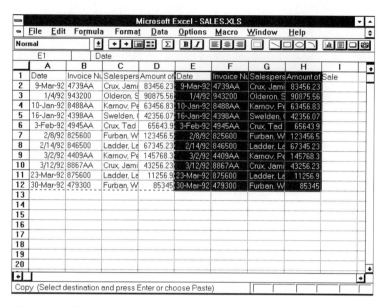

2. Select cell E1, and choose Paste from the Edit menu.

   Notice that you do not have to select a range of cells in which to paste the copied range. Excel assumes that the selected cell is the location of the top-left corner of the paste area. Also notice that the marquee still surrounds the original selection, indicating that you can paste another copy of the entries if necessary, even though the range E1:H12 is now selected.

3. Select cell F1, and choose Paste from the Edit menu. Again, Excel uses the selected cell as the top-left corner of the paste area and, without warning, pastes the entries over the existing contents of cells F1:I12.

Undoing commands

Cause for panic? Not at all. Excel's Undo command is designed for just such an occasion.

4. Choose Undo Paste from the Edit menu. Excel restores your worksheet to its prepaste status.

5. Select cell E1, and choose Insert Paste from the Edit menu. Excel displays this dialog box:

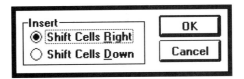

Choosing the Insert Paste command tells Excel to paste in the copied range, inserting enough cells to accommodate the entries without overwriting any existing cell contents. Excel wants to know in which direction it should move the existing cells, guessing that you will want to move them to the right because the copied range has more rows than columns.

6. Click OK. Excel proceeds with the paste operation, inserting a second copy of A1:D12 between the original and the first copy, as shown here:

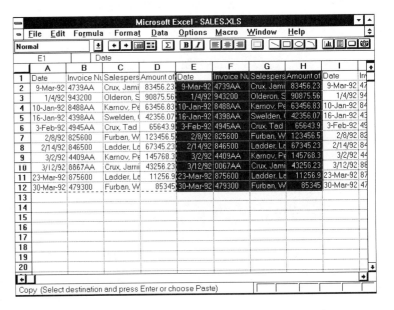

Notice that the first copy of the range has shifted to cells I1:L12. The marquee still surrounds the original range, so let's make yet another copy, this time in Sheet2.

1. Choose Sheet2 from the bottom of the Window menu, and check that cell A1 is active.
2. Choose Paste from the Edit menu. Excel faithfully pastes in a copy of the range from SALES.XLS.

Moving Entries

The procedure for moving cell entries is almost identical to that for copying entries. Again, you use two commands: Cut and Paste (or Insert Paste). Try this:

1. Choose Arrange All from the Window menu to display both open worksheets.
2. Activate SALES.XLS, and use the bottom scroll bar to move columns E:H into view. Select the range E1:H12 of SALES.XLS, and choose Cut from the Edit menu. Again, Excel surrounds the selection with a marquee.
3. Select cell A13 of Sheet2, and choose Paste from the Edit menu. Excel moves the entries from E1:H12 of SALES.XLS into A13:D24 of Sheet2. Your worksheets now look like this:

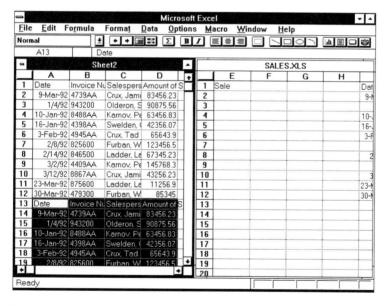

4. To get a better view of the results in SALES.XLS, activate the window, and click its Maximize button.
5. Pull down the Edit menu, and notice that the Paste command is gray and unavailable. Unlike copied entries, you can paste cut entries only once.

Clearing Cells

Now let's tidy up SALES.XLS by getting rid of the other copy of your data. You need to erase the entries in cells I1:L12—in Excel jargon, you need to *clear the cells*. Clearing entries is different from cutting them: Cutting assumes that you will paste the entries somewhere else, whereas clearing simply erases the entries. Here's how you clear cells:

1. Select the range I1:L12, and choose Clear from the Edit menu. Excel displays this dialog box:

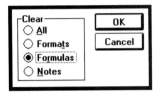

   The default option in the Clear dialog box is Formulas. For this type of operation, Excel considers all entries formulas, even plain text and numerical values that don't involve any computations. You can use the other options to clear any formats and notes that you have assigned to cells (see page 134), but in this case, the default option is just what you need.

2. Click OK. Excel clears the entries, and your worksheet now looks as it did before you started copying and moving.

Inserting and Deleting Cells

It is a rare person who can create a worksheet from scratch without ever having to tinker with its design—moving this block of data, changing that heading, or adding or deleting a column here and there. In this section, we'll show you how to insert and delete cells. Follow these steps:

Inserting columns →

1. Click the column D header to select the entire column.

2. Choose Insert from the Edit menu. Excel inserts an entire blank column in front of the Amount of Sale column, which as you can see here is now column E:

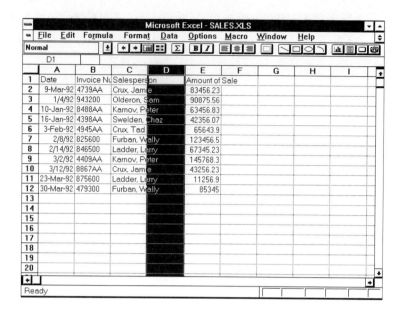

Inserting a row works exactly the same way as inserting a ←
column. You simply click the row header and choose Insert
from the Edit menu.

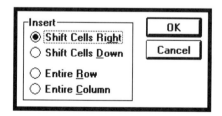

Inserting rows

What if you need to insert only a few cells and inserting an
entire column will mess up some of your entries? You can
insert cells anywhere you need them, as you'll see if you
follow these steps:

1. Select cells E1:E10—all but two of the cells containing
    amounts—and then choose Insert from the Edit menu.
    Excel displays this dialog box:

```
┌─Insert──────────┐  ┌──────────┐
│ ⦿ Shift Cells Right │  │    OK    │
│ ○ Shift Cells Down  │  ├──────────┤
│                     │  │  Cancel  │
│ ○ Entire Row        │  └──────────┘
│ ○ Entire Column     │
└─────────────────────┘
```

Because you have selected a range rather than the entire
column, Excel needs to know which cells to move to
make room for the inserted cells.

2. Click OK to accept the default option of shifting cells
    to the right. Excel inserts a new blank cell to the left of
    each selected cell, as shown on the next page.

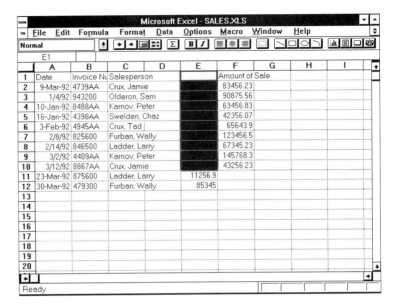

You could undo this insert to restore the integrity of the Amount of Sale column, but instead let's delete E1:E10:

1. With E1:E10 selected, choose the Delete command from the Edit menu. Excel displays a Delete dialog box similar to the Insert dialog box to find out how to close up the space that will be left by the deleted cells.

2. Click OK to accept the default option of shifting cells to the left. Excel deletes the cells, and the sale amounts are now back in one column.

You can leave the empty column D where it is for now—you'll use it when we work with SALES.XLS again in the next chapter.

Formatting Basics

Excel offers a wide variety of formatting options that allow you to emphasize parts of your worksheets and display data in different ways. Here we'll look at the formatting options that are available from the Toolbar, shown below:

We'll also show you a quick way to adjust column widths. Later, when you have more Excel experience, you might want to explore the formatting options available on the Format menu.

Changing Character Styles

Just as you can use headings to make tables of data easier to read, you can use styles to distinguish different categories of information. Styles change the appearance of the characters on the worksheet. For example, you might apply the bold style to major headings and the bold and italic styles to minor headings to make them stand out. Because these two character styles are the ones you will probably use most often, Excel has tools for them on the Toolbar. Try this:

Bold and italic

1. Click the header of row 1 to select the row containing your worksheet headings.
2. Click the Bold tool on the Toolbar. The headings are now bold, as shown here:

	Microsoft Excel									
	File	Edit	Formula	Format	Data	Options	Macro	Window	Help	

Normal

A1 | Date

	A	B	C	D	E	F	G	H	I
1	**Date**	**Invoice N**	**Salesperson**		**Amount of Sale**				
2	9-Mar-92	4739AA	Crux, Jamie		83456.23				
3	1/4/92	943200	Olderon, Sam		90875.56				
4	10-Jan-92	8488AA	Karnov, Peter		63456.83				
5	16-Jan-92	4398AA	Swelden, Chaz		42356.07				
6	3-Feb-92	4945AA	Crux, Tad		65643.9				
7	2/8/92	825600	Furban, Wally		123456.5				
8	2/14/92	846500	Ladder, Larry		67345.23				
9	3/2/92	4409AA	Karnov, Peter		145768.3				
10	3/12/92	8867AA	Crux, Jamie		43256.23				
11	23-Mar-92	875600	Ladder, Larry		11256.9				
12	30-Mar-92	479300	Furban, Wally		85345				
13									

The Toolbar tools

The Toolbar puts a variety of helpful worksheet tools at your fingertips. From left to right, here's what they do:

The Style tool allows you to create and apply cell formatting by selecting from the Style drop-down list box.

The Outlining tools include the Promote and Demote tools, which change outline levels, and the Outline tool which creates an outline.

The Select Visible Cells tool allows you to cut or copy part of a worksheet without affecting hidden rows or columns.

The Auto-sum tool inserts a SUM formula to add values above or to the left of the cell.

The Bold and Italic tools apply text formatting to cells.

The Alignment tools left-align, right-align, and center cell entries.

The Selection tool selects objects drawn with the Drawing tools.

The Drawing tools include the Line, Rectangle, Oval, and Arc tools, which allow you to create worksheet art.

The Chart tool allows you to create worksheet charts.

The Text tool allows you to annotate worksheets with boxed text.

The Button tool allows you to create macro buttons.

The Camera tool takes a picture of selected cells. ♦

Because you have formatted the entire row, any entries you now make in row 1 will be bold. Although you can copy or cut and paste formatting along with entries, it is the cell that is actually formatted, not the entry.

Changing Alignment

As you know, by default Excel left-aligns text and right-aligns numeric values. You can override the default alignment by using the Toolbar's Alignment tools:

Aligning entries

1. Check that row 1 is still selected.
2. Click each Alignment tool in the Toolbar, noting its effect. Finish by clicking the Center Alignment tool, which is the usual choice for headings.

Changing Column Widths

As the finishing touch to your first worksheet, you'll want to adjust the widths of columns B, C, and E so that the column headings fit neatly in their cells. Here's what you do:

Manual adjustment

1. Move the mouse pointer to the dividing line between the header of column B and that of column C. The pointer shape changes to a vertical bar with two opposing arrows:

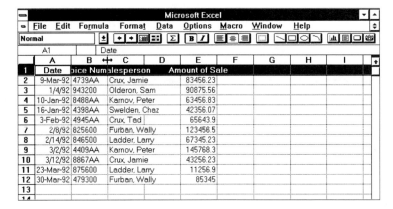

2. Hold down the mouse button, and drag to the right until column B is wide enough to display the Invoice Number heading. Notice that the width of the column is

displayed at the left end of the formula bar as you drag the border. (The standard column width is a little over 8 characters—8.43 to be exact.) Release the mouse button when you think that the text will fit into the cell.

Now widen columns C and E using a different method:

1. Click the column C header and hold down Ctrl while you click column E. Both columns are now selected.

2. Choose Column Width from the Format menu. Excel displays this dialog box:

Using the Column Width command

Because you have not adjusted the widths of columns C and E before, 8.43—the standard width—is displayed in the Column Width text box.

3. Click Best Fit, and then click OK. Excel increases the widths of the columns so that the column headings and values are displayed in their entirety.

Your finished worksheet looks like this:

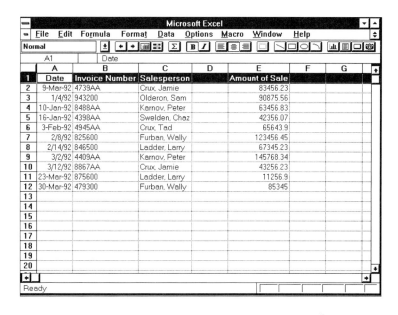

Adjusting row height

You can adjust the height of rows the same way you adjust the width of columns. Simply drag the bottom border of the row header up or down or choose Row Height from the Format menu to make the row shorter or taller.

Getting Help

This tour of Excel has covered a lot of ground in a few pages, and you might be wondering how you will manage to retain it all. Don't worry. If you forget how to carry out a particular task, help is never far away. For example, let's see how you would remind yourself of how to save a worksheet:

Context-sensitive help

1. Highlight the Save command on the File menu, and without releasing the mouse button, press F1. Excel displays this Help screen:

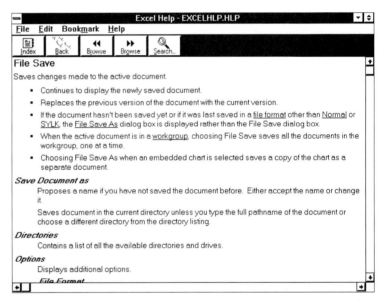

2. Click the Index button to display a list of topics, which provide information on almost every aspect of Excel.
3. Double-click the Control-menu icon in the top-left corner to close the Help Index.

Quitting Excel

Well, that's it for the basic tour. All that's left is to show you how to end an Excel session. Here's how:

1. Choose Exit from the File menu.
2. When Excel asks whether you want to save the changes you have made to the open worksheets, click Yes for SALES.XLS, and click No for Sheet2.

2

Analyzing Income

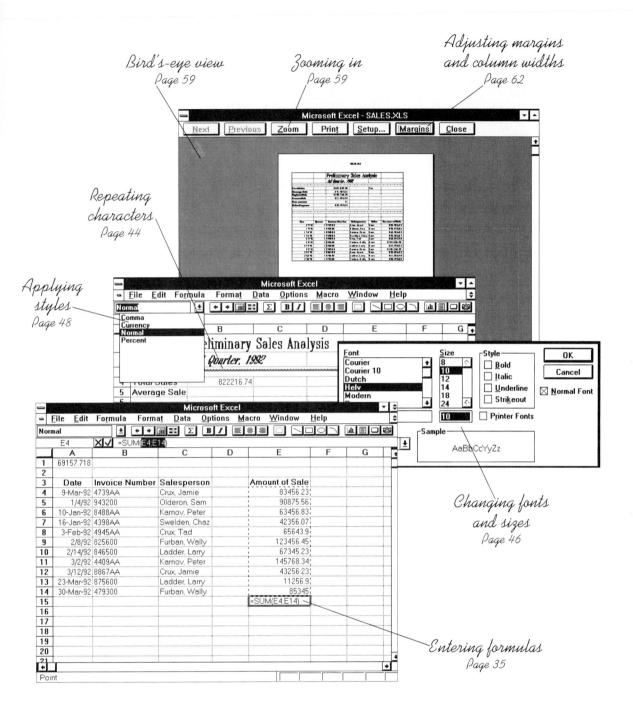

Bird's-eye view
Page 59

Zooming in
Page 59

*Adjusting margins
and column widths*
Page 62

*Repeating
characters*
Page 44

*Applying
styles*
Page 48

*Changing fonts
and sizes*
Page 46

Entering formulas
Page 35

Chapter 1 covered some Excel basics, and you now know enough to create simple tables. But you are missing the essential piece of information that turns a table into a worksheet: how to enter formulas. The whole purpose of building worksheets is to have Excel perform calculations for you. In this chapter, we show you how to retrieve the SALES.XLS worksheet and enter often-used formulas to analyze sales. (If you don't work in sales, you can adapt the worksheet to analyze other sources of income.) Along the way, you learn some powerful techniques for manipulating your data, and we cover the principles of worksheet design. Finally, we print the SALES.XLS worksheet. So fire up Excel, and we'll get started.

Opening Existing Worksheets

When you first start Excel, the worksheet window contains a blank document entitled Sheet1. You can open a worksheet you have already created in a couple of ways. If the worksheet is one of the last four you have worked with, you can simply choose the file from the bottom of the File menu. Otherwise, you can use the Open command, also on the File menu, to retrieve the worksheet. We'll use the first method:

Closing worksheets

1. If a blank Sheet1 is displayed on your screen, conserve your computer's memory by closing it. Simply double-click the Control-menu box in the top-left corner of the window, or choose Close from the File menu.
2. Now pull down the File menu, and choose SALES.XLS from the bottom of the menu. Excel displays the table you created in Chapter 1.
3. Click the worksheet's Maximize button to make it as large as possible.

Simple Calculations

Excel has many powerful functions that are a sort of shorthand for the various formulas used in mathematical, statistical, financial, trigonometric, logical, logarithmic, and other types of calculations. However, the majority of worksheets created with Excel involve simple arithmetic. In this section, we show you how to use the four arithmetic operators (+, –, *, and /) to add, subtract, multiply, and divide, and then we introduce two Excel features with which you can quickly add sets of numeric values.

Doing Arithmetic

You must begin all formulas you enter in Excel with an equal sign (=). In the simplest formulas, the equal sign is followed by a set of values separated by +, –, *, or /, such as

=5+3+2

If you enter this formula in any blank cell in your worksheet, Excel displays the result 10.

Let's experiment with a few formulas. We'll start by inserting a couple of blank rows:

1. Click the header of row 1 and drag down to row 2 to select both rows.   *Inserting rows*
2. Choose Insert from the Edit menu. Excel inserts two blank rows above the table, moving the table down so that it begins in row 3.

Now we're ready to construct a formula in cell A1, using some of the values in the Amount of Sale column. We could retype these values into the formula bar to create the formula, but instead we'll tell Excel to use a value simply by clicking the cell that contains it. Follow these steps:

1. Click cell A1, and type an equal sign followed by an opening parenthesis.   *Entering formulas*
2. Click cell E4. Excel inserts the reference E4 in the formula bar.
3. Type a plus sign, and click cell E5. Excel adds the reference E5 to the formula.
4. Continue to build the formula by typing plus signs and clicking cells E6, E7, and E8.
5. Type a closing parenthesis followed by a /—the division operator—and then type 5. The formula bar now looks like this:

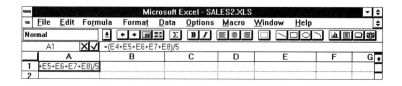

This formula tells Excel to first add the amounts in cells E4, E5, E6, E7, and E8 and then divide the result by 5, to obtain the average of the five amounts.

6. Click the Enter box. Excel displays the result of the formula, 69157.718, in cell A1.

You can use the same technique to create any simple formula. You simply type an equal sign, then type a value or click the cell that contains the value, type the appropriate arithmetic operator, enter the next value, and so on. Excel performs multiplication and division before addition and subtraction. If you need parts of the formula to be carried out in a specific order, use parentheses as we did in the previous calculation to override the default order.

Totaling Columns of Values

Although this method of creating a formula is simple enough, it would be tedious to have to type and click to create long formulas. Fortunately, Excel automates the process of totaling a series of numeric values with a very useful tool: the Auto-sum tool on the Toolbar.

Using the Auto-sum Tool   The Auto-sum tool will probably become your most often-used Excel tool.

Auto-sum tool

Using this tool is so easy that we'll dispense with explanations and simply show you how:

1. Click cell E15 to select it, and then click the Auto-sum tool. Excel looks above and to the left of the active cell for the largest range of numeric values to total. Because there are no values to the left of cell E15, Excel assumes that you want to total the values above it. Excel then enters a SUM function in cell E15. (We discuss the SUM function next.) Your worksheet now looks like this:

```
 ═══════════════════════════ Microsoft Excel ═══════════════ ▼ ▲
 ⊖  File  Edit  Formula  Format  Data  Options  Macro  Window  Help    ▲
 Normal         ▲ ← → ▦ ▦ Σ  B I  ≣ ≣ ≣  ▢ ⟍▢◯⟍ ▥▤▢▦
        E4      X √  =SUM(E4:E14)
        A         B              C         D        E        F        G    ▲
  1  69157.718
  2
  3  Date     Invoice Number Salesperson          Amount of Sale
  4  9-Mar-92 4739AA         Crux, Jamie             83456.23
  5  1/4/92   943200         Olderon, Sam            90875.56
  6  10-Jan-92 8488AA        Karnov, Peter           63456.83
  7  16-Jan-92 4398AA        Swelden, Chaz           42356.07
  8  3-Feb-92 4945AA         Crux, Tad               65643.9
  9  2/8/92   825600         Furban, Wally          123456.45
 10  2/14/92  846500         Ladder, Larry           67345.23
 11  3/2/92   4409AA         Karnov, Peter          145768.34
 12  3/12/92  8867AA         Crux, Jamie             43256.23
 13  23-Mar-92 875600        Ladder, Larry           11256.9
 14  30-Mar-92 479300        Furban, Wally           85345
 15                                            =SUM(E4:E14)
 16
 17
 18
 19
 20
 21                                                                    ▼
 ◄                                                                   ► 
 Point
```

2. Click the Enter box to record the function in cell E15.
   Excel displays the result of the function, 822216.74—
   the total of the range E4:E14.

Well, that was easy. The Auto-sum tool will serve you well
whenever you want a total to appear at the bottom of a
column or to the right of a row of numeric values. But what
if you want the total to appear elsewhere on the worksheet?
Knowing how to create SUM functions from scratch gives
you more flexibility.

Using the SUM Function   Let's go back and dissect the SUM
function that Excel inserted in cell E15 when you clicked the
Auto-sum tool, so that you can see the function's components. Clicking cell E15 puts this entry in the formula bar:

   =SUM(E4:E14)

Like all formulas, the SUM function begins with an equal
sign. Next comes the function name in capital letters, followed by a set of parentheses enclosing the reference of the
range containing the amounts you want to total. This reference is the SUM function's argument. An argument answers
questions such as "What?" or "How?" and gives Excel the
additional information it needs to perform the function. In
the case of SUM, Excel needs only one piece of information—the references of the cells you want it to total. As you'll
see later in this chapter, Excel might need several pieces of

◄——— Function syntax

information to carry out other functions, and you enter an argument for each piece.

Creating a SUM formula from scratch is not particularly difficult. To see how, follow these steps:

1. Select cell A1, and type this:

    =SUM(

    When you select a cell and begin typing, any value already in the cell is overwritten.

2. Select E4:E14. Excel inserts the range reference after the opening parenthesis.

3. Type a closing parenthesis.

4. Click the Enter box. Excel displays in cell A1 the total of the numeric values in the Amount of Sale column—822216.7. Because the widths of cells A1 and E15 are different, their displayed results appear slightly different, but their underlying values are identical.

Using References to Formula Cells in Other Formulas

After you create a formula in one cell, you can use its result in other formulas simply by referencing its cell. To see how this works, follow these steps:

1. Select cell B1, and type an equal sign.

2. Click cell A1, which contains the SUM function you just entered, type a / (the division operator), and then type *11*.

Function names	Parenthesis check	Displaying formulas
When you type a function name such as SUM in the formula bar, you don't have to type it in capital letters. Excel capitalizes the function name for you when you finish entering the function. If Excel doesn't respond in this way, you have probably entered the function name or its syntax incorrectly. ♦	When you enter a function's closing parenthesis, Excel briefly makes the pair of parentheses bold in the formula bar to tell you that you have a matching pair. When you enter long formulas or equations with multiple sets of parentheses, if you inadvertently forget to include a required parenthesis, this simple warning system alerts you to the problem. ♦	By default, Excel displays the results of formulas in cells, not the underlying formulas. To see the underlying formulas in the worksheet, choose Display from the Options menu, select the Formulas option, and click OK. Excel widens the cells so that you can view the formulas. Simply select the Formulas option again to redisplay the results. ♦

3. Click the Enter box. Excel displays the result—the average of the invoice amounts—in cell B1.

(We discuss an easier way to calculate averages on page 51.)

Naming Cells and Ranges

Many of the calculations that you might want to perform on this worksheet—for example, calculating each invoice amount as a percentage of total sales—will use the total you have just entered in cell A1. You could include a copy of the SUM function now in cell A1 in these other calculations, or you could simply reference cell A1. The latter method seems quick and simple, but what if you subsequently move the formula in cell A1 to another location. Excel gives you a way to reference this formula, no matter where you move it. You can assign cell A1 a name and then use the name in any calculations that involve the total.

You assign a name to a cell with the Define Name command on the Formula menu. Follow these steps:

1. Select cell A1, and choose Define Name from the Formula menu. Excel displays this dialog box: *Defining names*

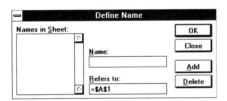

The reference for cell A1 is displayed in the Refers To text box with dollar signs in front of its column and row components. These dollar signs tell Excel that the cell reference is absolute, meaning that you will be able to use the name to refer to cell A1 from anywhere on the worksheet. (We discuss relative and absolute cell references later in this chapter, on page 58.)

2. Type the name *Total* in the Name box, and click OK.

To see how Excel uses names, try this:

1. Click cell E15, which currently contains the SUM function inserted when you clicked the Auto-sum tool earlier in the chapter.   *Using names*

2. Type =*Total*, and press Enter to record the entry in the cell. The worksheet does not appear to have changed, but now instead of two SUM functions, the worksheet contains only one: You have told Excel to assign the value of the cell named Total, which contains the SUM function, to cell E15.

You can also assign names to cell ranges. Let's assign the name Amount_of_Sale to the cells containing amounts in column E. You could select the range E4:E14, choose Define Name, and type the name in the Name text box, but here's an easier way:

1. Select E3:E14, and choose Create Names from the Formula menu. Excel displays this dialog box:

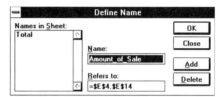

Excel scans the range and guesses that you want to assign the heading, Amount_of_Sale, above the range as its name. (Notice that in the name, Excel replaces the spaces in the heading with underscore characters.)

2. Click OK to assign the name.

Cell-naming conventions

Certain rules apply when you name cells or ranges. Although you can use a number within the name, you must start the name with a letter. Also, spaces are not allowed within the name. Use underscore characters (_) to represent any spaces. For example, you cannot use 1991 as a name, but you can use Totals_1991. ♦

Unique names

If you create a table with column headings across the top and row headings in the leftmost column, you can tell Excel to give each cell a unique name by combining the column and row headings. Select the entire table, choose Create Names from the Formula menu, select the Top Row and Left Column options, and click OK. ♦

Linking with names

You can use names to refer to cells and ranges on other worksheets, even ones that are not currently open. See page 118 for more information about linking worksheets in this way. ♦

Now let's replace the range reference in the SUM function in cell A1 with the new range name:

1. Click cell A1 to select it and display its contents in the formula bar.
2. Drag through the E4:E14 reference to highlight it.
3. Choose Paste Name from the Formula menu. Excel displays this dialog box:

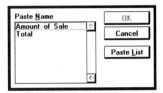

Pasting names

4. Select Amount_of_Sale from the Paste Name list box, and click OK. The name replaces the range reference in the SUM function.
5. Click the Enter box. The total in cell A1 remains the same because the name Amount_of_Sale and the reference E4:E14 both refer to the same range.

Efficient Data Display

Before we take a look at some of the other calculations you might want to perform with this worksheet, let's pause for a moment to look at ways to format your information to make it easier to read at a glance. We'll show you how to make the results of your calculations stand out from your data and how to format the data itself so that it is neat and consistent. As your worksheets grow in complexity, you'll find that paying attention to such details will keep you oriented and help others understand your results.

Creating a Calculation Area

Usually when you create a worksheet, you are interested not so much in the individual items of data as in the results of the calculations you perform on the items. The worksheet you are working with now fits neatly on one screen, but often worksheets of this type include several screenfuls of information. It's a good idea to design your worksheets so that the important information is easily accessible, and it helps if this information is always in a predictable location. For these reasons, we leave room in the top-left corner of our worksheets for a calculation area. This habit is useful for the following reasons:

- We don't have to scroll around looking for column and row totals and other results because we always know where to look for them.
- We can print just the first page of the worksheet to get a report of the most pertinent information.
- We can easily jump to the calculation area from anywhere on the worksheet by pressing Ctrl-Home to move to cell A1.

Let's create an area at the top of the SALES.XLS worksheet for a title and a set of calculations now. When we've finished, the worksheet will look like this:

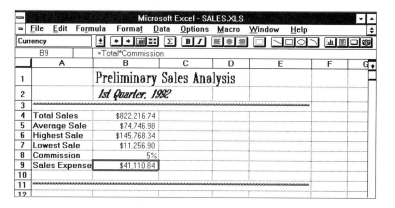

We'll start by adding several more rows at the top of the worksheet to accommodate the calculation area. Let's try a different insertion method:

1. Select the range A1:E14, and choose Cut from the Edit menu. The range is now surrounded by a marquee.
2. Select cell A10, and choose Paste from the Edit menu. Excel picks up the entire range and moves it down to A10:E23, as shown on the facing page.

```
┌─────────────────────────────────────────────────────────────────────┐
│ ─                    Microsoft Excel - SALES.XLS              ▼ ▲     │
│ ─  File  Edit  Formula  Format  Data  Options  Macro  Window  Help ▲│
│ Normal        ± ◄ ► ▦ ▦ Σ  B I  ≡ ≡ ≡  □ ◜◻◯◟ ⊞▣▢☺           │
│     A10              =SUM(Amount_of_Sale)                             │
│     A          B              C         D        E       F      G    │
│  5                                                                    │
│  6                                                                    │
│  7                                                                    │
│  8                                                                    │
│  9                                                                    │
│ 10  822216.7                                                          │
│ 11                                                                    │
│ 12  Date    Invoice Number  Salesperson      Amount of Sale          │
│ 13  9-Mar-92 4739AA         Crux, Jamie          83456.23            │
│ 14  1/4/92   943200         Olderon, Sam         90875.56            │
│ 15 10-Jan-92 8488AA         Karnov, Peter        63456.83            │
│ 16 16-Jan-92 4398AA         Swelden, Chaz        42356.07            │
│ 17  3-Feb-92 4945AA         Crux, Tad            65643.9             │
│ 18  2/8/92   825600         Furban, Wally       123456.45            │
│ 19  2/14/92  846500         Ladder, Larry        67345.23            │
│ 20  3/2/92   4409AA         Karnov, Peter       145768.34            │
│ 21  3/12/92  8867AA         Crux, Jamie          43256.23            │
│ 22 23-Mar-92 875600         Ladder, Larry        11256.9             │
│ 23 30-Mar-92 479300         Furban, Wally        85345               │
│ 24                                                                    │
│ Ready                                                                 │
└─────────────────────────────────────────────────────────────────────┘
```

As you can see, Excel can handle overlapping cut and paste areas without garbling the results.

Now let's enter the worksheet title:

1. Scroll to cell B1, select it, and type *Preliminary Sales Analysis*.

2. Select cell B2 and type *1st Quarter, 1992*.

Next, we'll set off the calculation area. With Excel 3, you can get really fancy, using borders and shading to draw attention to calculation results. In Chapter 6, we show you some special techniques for formatting your worksheets. For

---

Avoiding pasting over cells

Notice that the formula that was in cell E15 has been overwritten by the pasted cells. Because it was not part of the cut range, the formula is lost. In this case, the loss is not important. However, you can avoid inadvertently overwriting critical information during a cut-and-paste operation by using the Insert Paste command instead of the Paste command. After you indicate in the Insert Paste dialog box how you want it to make room for the range you are moving, Excel pastes it into its new location, shifting rows or columns as necessary. See page 22 for more information about the Insert Paste command. ♦

Moving formulas

The formula now in cell A10 remains correct, even though you have moved it. A distinct advantage of using named references and relative references in a formula is that you can move the formula without disturbing the results. ♦

now, though, let's draw lines of asterisks above and below the area, using one of Excel's special alignment formats.

Repeating characters

1. Select cell A3, type one asterisk, and then click the Enter box.

2. Now select cells A3:E3, and choose the Alignment command from the Format menu. Excel displays this dialog box:

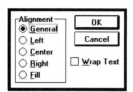

3. Select the Fill option, and click OK. Here's the result:

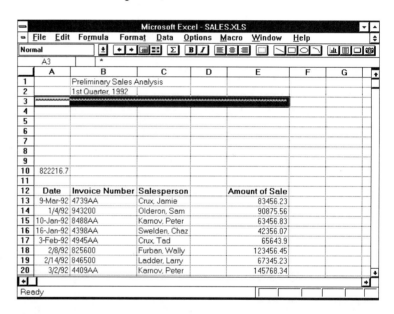

4. Create the bottom line of asterisks by repeating steps 1 through 3 for cell A9 and the range A9:E9.

Now that we have created a calculation area, let's move the calculation in cell A10. Follow these steps:

1. Select cell A4, type Total Sales, and then click the Enter box.

2. Select cell A10, and choose Cut from the Edit menu.

3. Select cell B4, and choose Paste from the Edit menu.

4. Select A4:A8, and click the Bold tool on the Toolbar. Here's the result:

Why did we tell you to select the empty cells below the Total Sales label before applying the bold format? Try this:

1. Select cell A5, and type *Average Sale*. The new label is bold, because we have already applied the bold format to cell A5.

2. Use any of the techniques you learned in Chapter 1 to widen column A so that you can see both the labels you have entered. From now on, adjust the column widths as necessary to see your work.

Other repeating characters

You can use the Fill option to repeat any character or group of characters so that they fill a single cell or a range of cells. Some common examples of other repeating characters are hyphens and equal signs. You might also want to experiment with combinations, such as hyphen-space-asterisk, to create different effects. ◆

Flexible fill

Using the Fill option is more efficient than typing countless characters, not only because it saves typing time but also because the Fill option responds to changes you make to column widths. For example, if you decrease the width of column A, Excel simply adjusts the number of asterisks accordingly, so that they continue to fill ranges A3:E3 and A9:E9. ◆

Optical illusion

If you click the cells in columns B through E that appear to contain asterisks, you will see that they are empty. The only asterisk is the single one you typed in column A. If you enter another character in any of these cells, Excel repeats the character in that cell and in all cells to the right of it that have the Fill format. ◆

Formatting Text

In Chapter 1, you learned how to format text in simple ways—using the tools on the Toolbar to change alignment and make text bold or italic. In this section, we'll get a bit more elaborate and show you how to change the font of the worksheet title and make it bigger so that it really stands out. Here's how:

Changing fonts and sizes

1. Select cell B1, and choose Font from the Format menu. Excel displays this dialog box:

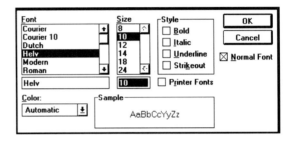

2. Select Roman in the Font list box, 18 in the Size list box, and Bold in the Style section. Click OK. Notice that the height of row 1 increases to accommodate the larger font.
3. Select cell B2, and choose Font from the Format menu.
4. Select Roman in the Font list box, 14 in the Size list box, and both Bold and Italic in the Style section. Click OK. Here's the effect of your changes:

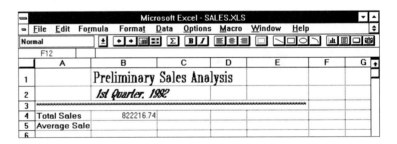

Displaying Dollars and Cents

Excel has displayed all the numeric values you've entered so far in its default General format, which right-aligns them but does not change their appearance. With the General format, Excel simply displays what you typed (or what it thinks you typed). However, Excel provides several formats that do change the way the values look. The three other formats you are likely to use most often are gathered together in the Style drop-down list box at the left end of the Toolbar, as shown here:

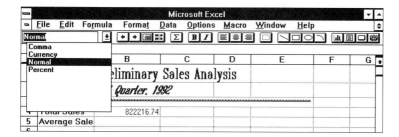

These styles produce the following effects:

- The Normal style is the General format and the default font and size. You can add font, alignment, and other formats to define Normal to suit your needs. (See page 130 for information about defining styles.)
- The Comma style inserts commas to group the digits in values greater than 999 into threes.
- The Currency style adds a dollar sign in front of the value, uses commas to group the digits by threes, and displays two decimal places (cents).
- The Percent style displays the value as a percentage and appends a percent sign.

Preformatting for efficiency

Formatting blank cells is an efficient way to build a worksheet. For example, if you know that a block of cells will contain the dollar-value result of a formula, you can preformat the entire block. ♦

Font list

The fonts that are listed in the Font dialog box depend on several factors, including the resolution of your screen, which fonts you have installed with Windows, and which additional printer fonts you have purchased and installed (if any). ♦

Room to experiment

Use the Sample portion of the Font dialog box to experiment with combinations of font, size, and style before you apply the final format to the selected cell. ♦

Applying a style from the Style list box is a simple matter of selecting the cell or range you want to format and then selecting the desired style from the list box. Try this:

Applying styles →

1. Select B4:B8. (Again, you can save time by applying a style to a range, instead of to individual cells.)
2. Click the arrow to the right of Normal to display the available styles.
3. Select the Currency style by clicking it. The Style box closes, and Currency replaces Normal to indicate the style of the active cell. Your worksheet looks like this:

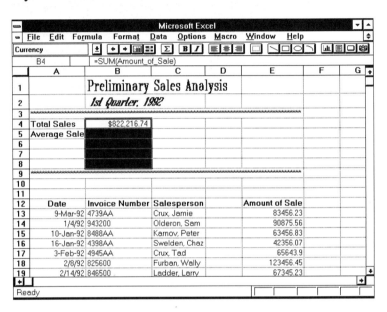

Entering in format

You can enter values into a cell "in format" instead of selecting a style from the Style list box or a format from the Format Number dialog box. For example, if you enter $12,345 into a cell and open the Format Number dialog box, you'll see that Excel has highlighted the $#,##0. format (currency with no decimal places). When you entered the dollar amount you also provided enough information to Excel to preformat it. If you had entered $12,345.67 instead, Excel would have recognized that the amount was formatted with the $#,##0.00 format. ♦

Underlying vs. displayed

After you apply a format, the value displayed in the cell might look different from the value in the formula bar. For example, 345.6789 is displayed in its cell as $345.68 if you apply the Currency style. When performing calculations, Excel will use the value in the formula bar, called the underlying value, not the displayed value. ♦

4. Without changing the active cell, choose Number from the Format menu. Excel displays this dialog box:

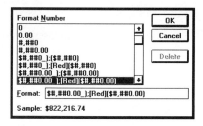

Number formats

The set of characters Excel has highlighted in the list box is its representation of the format that you have just applied to cell B4. The part of the format in front of the semicolon (;) is for positive numbers, and the part after the semicolon is for negative numbers, which will be displayed in parentheses (and in red on a color monitor).

The format tells Excel to display a dollar sign ($) followed by the value (#,##0.00), using commas to group digits in threes and always displaying one digit to the left of the decimal point and two to the right. If the value is less than $1—for example, if it is 93 cents—Excel is to display $0.93, and if the value has no fractional part—for example, if it is exactly $1— Excel is to display $1.00. The Sample portion of the dialog box shows how the entry in the active cell will look with the selected format.

The _) part of the format tells Excel to shift positive values away from the right border of the cell by the amount of space necessary to hold a closing parenthesis. As a result, in a column containing both negative and positive values, all the values will be decimal-aligned. To test this effect, try the following:

5. Click Cancel to close the dialog box.

6. Select cell B5, type *–1234*, and click the Enter box. Turn the page to see the result.

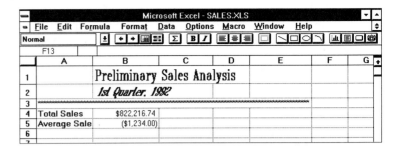

Excel displays the value in parentheses, aligning the value with the positive value above it and adding a dollar sign, a comma to separate hundreds from thousands, and two zeros to the right of the decimal point.

Now let's format the values in the Amount of Sale column as currency, this time using the Number command:

1. Select the range E13:E23, and choose Number from the Format menu.

2. Select the $#,##0.00_);($#,##0.00) format, and click the OK button.

Long numeric values

Don't worry if some of the cells display pound signs (#) instead of their values. With the addition of the commas and dollar signs, some of your numeric values might now be too long to fit in their cells. Excel replaces long currency values with pound signs (#), and you must make the cell wider to view them.

Formatting Dates

In Chapter 1, we entered dates in column A in a variety of formats. Now we'll show you how to change the date format to reflect the needs of your worksheet. Excel's date formats are grouped together with its time formats, at the bottom of the list in the Format Number dialog box. Let's experiment with the dates in column A:

1. Select the range A13:A23.

2. Choose Number from the Format menu to display the Format Number dialog box.

3. Scroll through the list box to bring the date formats into view, select the d-mmm format, and click OK. Here's the result:

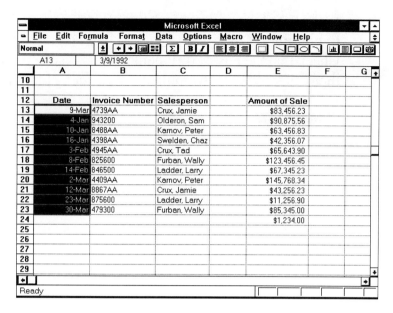

	A	B	C	D	E	F	G
10							
11							
12	Date	Invoice Number	Salesperson		Amount of Sale		
13	9-Mar	4739AA	Crux, Jamie		$83,456.23		
14	4-Jan	943200	Olderon, Sam		$90,875.56		
15	10-Jan	8488AA	Karnov, Peter		$63,456.83		
16	16-Jan	4398AA	Swelden, Chaz		$42,356.07		
17	3-Feb	4945AA	Crux, Tad		$65,643.90		
18	8-Feb	825600	Furban, Wally		$123,456.45		
19	14-Feb	846500	Ladder, Larry		$67,345.23		
20	2-Mar	4409AA	Karnov, Peter		$145,768.34		
21	12-Mar	8867AA	Crux, Jamie		$43,256.23		
22	23-Mar	875600	Ladder, Larry		$11,256.90		
23	30-Mar	479300	Furban, Wally		$85,345.00		
24					$1,234.00		
25							
26							
27							
28							
29							

4. Experiment with the other date formats to see their effects, and then apply the m/d/yy format.

More Calculations

Now we'll move back to the calculation area and perform some more calculations on the sales data, starting with the average sale.

Averaging Values

To find the average amount for the invoices we've entered in this worksheet, we'll use Excel's AVERAGE function. We'll also show you how to use the Paste Function command to avoid making errors while typing function names and to indicate the arguments necessary for Excel to calculate the function.

The AVERAGE function

1. Select cell B5, and choose Paste Function from the Formula menu. Excel displays this dialog box:

Pasting functions

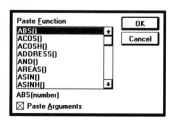

2. In the list of functions, scroll to AVERAGE(), and click to highlight it.

3. Check that the Paste Arguments option is selected, and then click OK. The formula bar now looks like this:

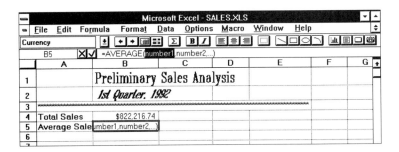

Notice that the argument *number1* is highlighted. To find the average of a series of numeric values, you could type the values in the formula bar in place of the argument names. In this example, you want to replace the first argument name with the reference of the range that contains the values you want to average, and then delete the other arguments.

4. Select the range E13:E23 to replace *number1*. Then highlight *,number2,...* and press the Del key to delete the extra argument. The formula bar looks like this:

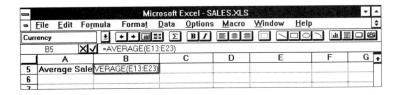

5. Click the Enter box to record the formula in cell B5. Excel displays the result: $74,746.98.

Identifying Highest and Lowest Sales

Excel provides two functions that instantly identify the highest and lowest values in a group. To understand the benefits of these functions, imagine that the SALES.XLS worksheet contains data from not 11 but 111 invoices! Let's start with the highest sale:

1. Select cell A6, type *Highest Sale*, and press Tab to enter the text and select cell B6.

2. Choose Paste Function from the Formula menu, and highlight MAX() in the list box.

The MAX function

3. This time, be sure that the Paste Arguments option is not selected so that you don't have to delete extraneous text from the formula bar. Then click OK. Excel pastes in only the function, with an insertion point between the open and close parentheses.

4. Select the range E13:E23, and click the Enter box. Excel enters the highest sale amount, $145,768.34, in cell B6.

Now for the formula for the lowest sale, which we'll type in the formula bar:

1. Select cell A7, type *Lowest Sale*, and press Tab.

2. Type *=MIN(E13:E23)*, and press Enter. Excel displays the result, $11,256.90, in cell A7

The MIN function

Calculating with Names

The last calculation we'll make with this set of data involves the Total Sales value from cell B4. As a gross indicator of sales expenses, let's calculate the total sales commission:

1. First, insert a couple of new rows in the calculation area by clicking the headers for rows 8 and 9 and choosing Insert from the Edit menu.

2. Select cell A8, type *Commission*, and press Tab.

3. Type *6%*, and click the Enter box. Excel displays $0.06, because the cell was formatted as currency. Six cents on the dollar is correct, but we want the value to appear as a percentage.

4. Select Percent from the Style list box on the Toolbar. Excel now displays 6%.

Formatting percents

5. With cell B8 still active, choose Define Name from the Formula menu. Excel scans the adjacent cells and suggests the name Commission. Click OK.

6. Select cell A9, type *Sales Expense*, and press Tab.

7. With cell B9 active, type *=Total*Commission*, and press Enter. Excel multiplies the value in the cell named Total (B4) by the value in the cell named Commission (B8) and displays the result, $49,333.00,

in cell B9. (The underlying value is 49333.0044, but Excel rounds it off.)

8. Now select cell B8, type *5%*, and press Enter. Instantly, the value in cell B9 changes to reflect the new commission rate, as shown here:

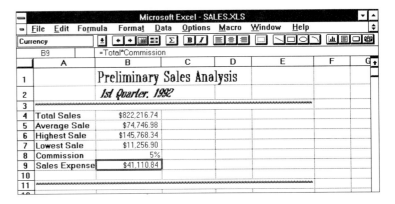

If a hundred calculations throughout the worksheet involved the name Commission, Excel would have adjusted all their results to reflect this one change. Powerful stuff!

Formulas That Make Decisions

There will be times when you want Excel to carry out one task under certain circumstances and another task if those circumstances don't apply. To give this kind of instruction to Excel, you use the IF function.

Using the IF Function

How IF works →

In it's simplest form, the IF function tests the value of a cell and does one thing if the test is positive (true) and another if the test is negative (false). It requires three arguments: the test, the action to perform if the test is true, and the action to perform if the test is false. You supply the arguments one after the other within the function's parentheses, separating them with commas (no spaces). Try this:

1. Select cell D4, type the following, and then click the Enter box:

=IF(B4=0,"TRUE","FALSE")

Excel checks whether the value of B4 is zero (the test), and because it isn't, it bypasses TRUE (the action to perform if the test is true) and displays FALSE (the action to perform if the test is false) in cell D4.

2. With cell D4 still selected, highlight =0 in the formula bar, type *<1000000*, and click the Enter box. The entry in cell D4 instantly changes from FALSE to TRUE, because the value in cell B4 is less than one million (in other words, the test is true).

In this example, the test Excel performed was a simple evaluation of the value in a cell. However, you can also build tests that involve other functions. Recall that the last two characters of the invoice numbers in column B of the worksheet indicate whether the sale originated in your company's East or West office. Suppose you want to assign East and West entries to each invoice so that you can compare the performance of the two offices. Follow these steps to experiment with a more complex IF example:

Functions in tests

1. Select cell D14, type *Office*, and press Enter. Excel centers the new column heading and displays it in bold, because the formats from the old column D were applied to the new column D when you inserted it.

2. In cell D15, type the following, and click the Enter box:

   =IF(RIGHT(B15,2)="AA","East","West")

The RIGHT function

Custom formats

You can create your own formats or modify an existing format to meet special formatting needs. A detailed discussion of creating custom formats could take an entire chapter, but here are the basic steps for creating a numeric format: Start by entering a number in a cell, and choose Number from the Format menu. Select a format that resembles the one you want to create. (If none of the formats is similar to the one you want, clear the Format text box, and start from scratch.) Use 0s as required digit placeholders and #s as optional digit placeholders. Use @ as a text placeholder. Also enter any text that you want to be part of the format, enclosing the text in quotation marks. For example, if the value is 123 and you want Excel to display *You owe me $123.00* in the cell, you would create this format:

   "You owe me " $##0.00

Custom formats exist only in the worksheet in which you create them. However, you can copy custom formats from one worksheet to another. You can also add custom formats to the Style list box and then merge the formats from one worksheet to another. ◆

You have told Excel to look at the two characters at the right end of the value in cell B15 and, if they are AA, to enter East in cell D15. If they are not AA, Excel is to enter West. Here's the result:

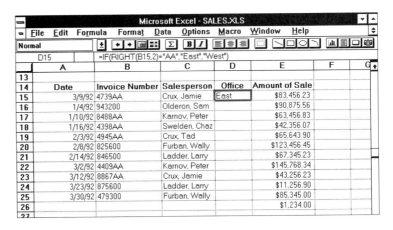

Using Nested IF Functions

Functions within functions

When constructing tests, you can use IF functions within IF functions. Called nested functions, these formulas add another dimension to the complexity of the decisions Excel can make. Here's a quick demonstration:

1. Insert a new column between columns A and B, and enter the column heading *Quarter* in cell B14.
2. Select cells B15:B25, choose Number from the Format menu, and apply the General format.

Logical operators

Here is a list of operators you can use with the IF function:

= < > <> >= <=

You can also use AND and OR to combine two or more tests. The function

=IF(AND(B4=0,B5>0),"Yes","No")

displays Yes only if both tests are true. The function

=IF(OR(B4=0,B5>0),"Yes","No")

displays Yes if either test is true. ♦

Text values as arguments

When entering text values as arguments in a formula, you must enclose them in quotation marks. Otherwise Excel thinks the text is a name and returns the #NAME? error value in the cell. ♦

A function for every task

Excel provides many functions for common business and financial tasks—some of them quite complex. Refer to the *Microsoft Excel Function Reference* that comes with the documentation for more information. ♦

3. Select cell B15 in the new column, and type the following on one line:

=IF(MONTH(A15)<4,1,IF(MONTH(A15)<7,2,
    IF(MONTH(A15)<10,3,4)))

4. Check your typing, paying special attention to all the parentheses, and then click the Enter box.

The MONTH function

You have told Excel to check the month component of the date in cell A15. If it is less than 4, Excel is to display 1 in the corresponding cell in the Quarter column. If the month is not less than 4 but is less than 7, Excel is to display 2 in the Quarter column. If it is not less than 7 but is less than 10, Excel is to display 3. Otherwise, Excel is to display 4. If you have typed the formula correctly, Excel enters 1 in cell B15.

Copying Formulas

The IF functions you have just entered are pretty arduous to type, even for good typists. Fortunately, you don't have to enter them more than once. With the Fill Down command on the Edit menu, you can copy the formulas into other cells.

1. Select B15:B25, and then choose Fill Down from the Edit menu.

Copying down a range

2. Select E15:E25, and choose Fill Down again.
3. Delete the formula you entered earlier in cell F26, and your worksheet now looks like this:

	Microsoft Excel - SALES.XLS					
File	Edit	Formula	Format	Data	Options	Macro	Window	Help

	A	B	C	D	E	F	G
13							
14	Date	Quarter	Invoice Number	Salesperson	Office	Amount of Sale	
15	3/9/92	1	4739AA	Crux, Jamie	East	$83,456.23	
16	1/4/92	1	943200	Olderon, Sam	West	$90,875.56	
17	1/10/92	1	8488AA	Karnov, Peter	East	$63,456.83	
18	1/16/92	1	4398AA	Swelden, Chaz	East	$42,356.07	
19	2/3/92	1	4945AA	Crux, Tad	East	$65,643.90	
20	2/8/92	1	825600	Furban, Wally	West	$123,456.45	
21	2/14/92	1	846500	Ladder, Larry	West	$67,345.23	
22	3/2/92	1	4409AA	Karnov, Peter	East	$145,768.34	
23	3/12/92	1	8867AA	Crux, Jamie	East	$43,256.23	
24	3/23/92	1	875600	Ladder, Larry	West	$11,256.90	
25	3/30/92	1	479300	Furban, Wally	West	$85,345.00	
26							
27							
28							
29							
30							
31							
32							

Ready

4. Select cell E15, and look at the formula in the formula bar. Excel has changed the original formula

=IF(RIGHT(B15,2)="AA","East","West")

to

=IF(RIGHT(C15,2)="AA","East","West")

Excel changed the reference to account for the addition of the Quarter column. If you click cell E16, you'll see that when you used Fill Down, Excel changed the reference so that it looks to cell C16, not C15.

Relative references →

By default, Excel uses relative references in its formulas. Relative references refer to cells by their position in relation to the cell containing the formula. So when you copied the formula in cell E15 to cell E16, Excel changed the reference in the formula from C15 to C16—the cell in the same row and two columns to the left of the cell containing the formula. If you were to copy the formula in cell E15 to F15, Excel would change the reference from C15 to D15 so that the formula would continue to reference the cell in the same relative position.

Absolute references →

When you don't want a reference to be copied as a relative reference, as it was in the preceding examples, you need to use an absolute reference. Absolute references refer to cells by their fixed position in the worksheet. To make a reference absolute, you add dollar signs before its column letter and row number. For example, to change the reference C4:C9 to an absolute reference, you would enter it as $C$4:$C$9. You could then move a formula that contained this reference anywhere on the worksheet and it would always refer to the range C4:C9.

To complicate matters, references can also be partially relative and partially absolute. For example, $C3 has an absolute column reference and a relative row reference, and C$3 has a relative column reference and an absolute row reference.

Printing Your Worksheets

If your primary purpose in learning Excel is to be able to manipulate your own information and come up with results that will guide your decision-making, your worksheets might never need to leave your computer. If, on the other hand, you want to sway the decisions of your colleagues or you need to prepare reports for your board of directors, you will probably need printed copies of your worksheets. Now is a good time to cover how to print an Excel document.

Previewing Worksheets

Usually, you will want to preview your worksheets before you print them to make sure that single-page documents fit neatly on the page and that multi-page documents break in logical places. Print Preview gives you a bird's-eye view of your document. You can change margins, column widths, and the basic page layout from this view, but you cannot make any modifications to the values in the worksheet. Let's preview SALES.XLS:

Bird's-eye view

1. Choose Print Preview from the File menu. The Print Preview window opens, with a miniature version of the printed page displayed.

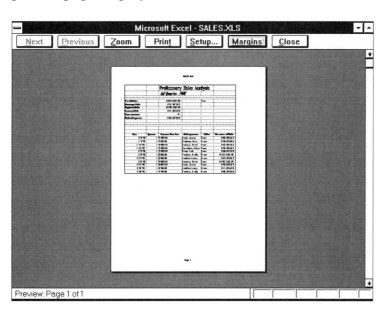

Notice that Excel will print only the rectangular block needed to hold all the cells containing entries.

2. Move the mouse pointer over the page. The pointer shape changes into a small magnifying glass.

3. To examine part of the page in more detail, move the magnifying glass over that part, and click the mouse button. Excel zooms in on that portion of the page.

Zooming in

Zooming out →

Click again to zoom out (or click the Zoom button at the top of the screen).

Setting Up the Pages

By default, Excel prints your worksheet with grid lines around each cell, the worksheet's filename as a header at the top of the page, and a page number as a footer at the bottom of the page. For presentation purposes, these default settings don't produce a very attractive printout, so you'll probably want to change them. You make these changes in the Page Setup dialog box, which Excel displays when you choose Page Setup from the File menu. When you are in Print Preview, you can also access this dialog box directly.

1. Click the Setup button at the top of the Print Preview window. Excel displays this Page Setup dialog box:

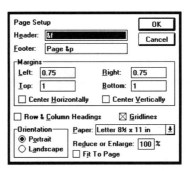

The Header and Footer text boxes contain codes that generate the default header and footer on the printed

---

Printer setup

If your computer can access more than one printer, or if you need to set up the printer to print with Excel, choose Printer Setup from the File menu, and make the necessary settings in the Printer dialog box before trying to print. ♦

Printer fonts vs. screen fonts

Always change Excel's default font, and any other fonts that you use on your worksheets, to one that is available on your printer. Although Excel and Windows may provide screen fonts that allow you to view text formatted with fonts not available on your printer, these fonts don't provide enough information to your printer to print correctly. ♦

Best Fit and fonts

If you use the Best Fit option in the Column Width dialog box to adjust column width, Excel may not print the worksheet correctly. Excel uses the screen font to adjust column width, and this font may differ slightly from the printer font. Use Print Preview each time you print to identify columns that are too narrow to hold numbers (they contain # signs). ♦

page. The code &f prints the filename as the header, and Page &p prints the word *Page* followed by the page number as the footer.

2. In the Header text box, type *&bSales Analysis*. The &b tells Excel to print *Sales Analysis* in bold.

3. Click the Footer text box, drag through Page &p to highlight it, and press the Del key to delete the footer.

4. Click the Center Horizontally and Center Vertically options.

5. Click the Gridlines option to turn it off, and then click OK. You return to the Print Preview window, which now looks like this:

Creating headers and footers

Page centering

Turning off gridlines

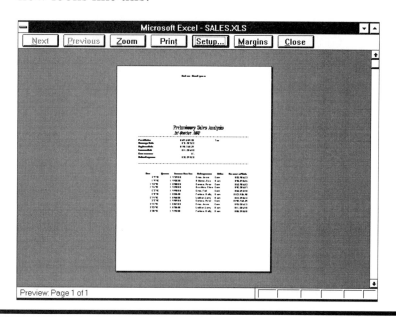

Printing on one page

Often, you can force Excel to print a worksheet on one page by manipulating the margins and widths of columns. You might also be able to use Reduce Or Enlarge and Fit To Page options in the Page Setup dialog box. (This dialog box is printer-specific and not all options will be available for all printers.) ◆

Header and footer codes

Here's a list of some of the header and footer codes you are most likely to use:

&d   Date
&t   Time
&f   Filename
&p   Page number
&l   Left-aligns following characters
&c   Centers following characters
&r   Right-aligns following characters

&b   Prints following characters in bold
&i   Prints following characters in italic
&u   Underlines following characters ◆

Adjusting margins and column widths →

You can adjust the margins and column widths of your printout directly from the Print Preview window by clicking the Margins button to display guidelines, and then manually moving the guidelines to increase or decrease the margins.

If you need to return to the worksheet to make additional changes before printing, you can close the Print Preview window by clicking the Close button.

Getting Ready to Print

When you are ready to print, you can simply choose the Print command from the File menu if you are in the regular document window, or you can print directly from the Print Preview window by following these steps:

1. Click the Print button in the Print Preview window. Excel displays the Print dialog box for your printer. (This dialog box is also displayed when you choose Print from the File menu.) Here's an example of this dialog box for a PostScript printer:

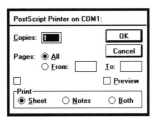

Setting page breaks

If you want to print the calculation area on one page and the supporting data on another, or if you need to control where the pages break in a multi-page worksheet, select the cell below the row and to the right of the column at which you want Excel to break the page, and choose the Set Page Break command from the Options menu. ◆

Removing page breaks

To remove a manual page break, select the cell immediately below and to the right of the page break, and choose Remove Page Break from the Options menu. ◆

Repeating headings

To repeat column headings on all pages of a multi-page worksheet, highlight the headings, and choose Set Print Titles from the Options menu. Then select all the cells of the worksheet below the headings, and choose Set Print Area from the Options menu. ◆

Because the Print dialog box varies for different printers, we'll keep our instructions here very general.

2. In the Copies text box, enter the number of copies you want to print.

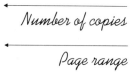

Number of copies

Page range

3. If you want to print the entire worksheet, leave the Pages option set to All. Otherwise, indicate the desired pages in the From and To edit boxes.

4. Check that the Preview option is not selected. (Selecting this option is another way to display the Print Preview window.)

5. Check that your printer is turned on and ready to go, and then click OK.

That should do it. We've done a lot of work in this chapter, and you can now evaluate the results on paper.

3

Extracting Information from a Database

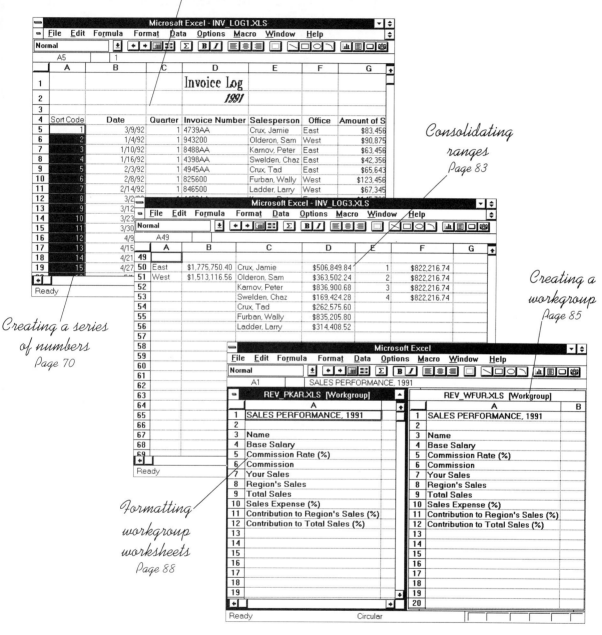

Opening a copy of
a template
Page 69

Consolidating
ranges
Page 83

Creating a
workgroup
Page 85

Creating a series
of numbers
Page 70

Formatting
workgroup
worksheets
Page 88

We covered a lot of important ground in Chapter 2, and you now have a feel for some of the power of Excel. In this chapter, we show you more techniques for efficient worksheet creation and management. Using an invoice log as a base worksheet, we describe how to create reusable templates, how to sort and extract data, and how to consolidate totals. While we're at it, we will show you a technique for working with several worksheets at the same time, and we link some worksheets to the master invoice log so that they are updated when the information in the log changes. Let's start by creating the invoice log.

Cloning Worksheets

Using one worksheet as the basis for another is an important time-saving technique. In this section, we will clone the SALES.XLS worksheet to create another worksheet called INV_LOG.XLS. Then we use a few tricks to transform the new worksheet into a simulated invoice log (a record of sales). If you need to create such a log for your work, you can key in real data. In Chapter 6, we show you how to automate the process of inputting this kind of information so that you are spared hours of typing. In the meantime, though, let's create a simulated log to give us a large worksheet to manipulate in the other sections of this chapter. Follow these steps to create INV_LOG.XLS:

Duplicating worksheets →

1. Use the Open command on the File menu to locate and open SALES.XLS.
2. Delete the extraneous formula in cell E4, and choose Save As from the File menu.
3. In the Save Worksheet As text box, type *inv_log*, and click OK.

You now have two nearly identical worksheets saved under different names. A few alterations to INV_LOG.XLS will give you a usable sample worksheet.

1. Select C1, type *Invoice Log*, and press Enter to both enter the text and select cell C2. Then type *1991*, and press Enter.
2. Select the headers for rows 3 through 12, and choose Delete from the Edit menu.

3. Select A5:F15, and choose Copy from the Edit menu.

4. Choose Insert Paste from the Edit menu, click the Shift Cells Down option, and click OK.

5. Select A5:F26, copy this range, and repeat step 4 to create a log containing 44 invoices.

Now, so that the log includes invoices for all the months of the year, follow these steps:

1. Select A16. Highlight 3 (the month) in the formula bar, type *4*, and press Enter. Excel displays the new date for this invoice and recalculates the formula in cell B16, assigning the invoice to the second quarter of the year instead of the first.

    Rather than changing dates manually for the rest of the worksheet, we'll take this opportunity to demonstrate the Series command on the Data menu. Later in this chapter, we'll use this command to create a sequential set of numbers. Here, we'll use it to create a set of evenly spaced dates. (If you were logging real invoices into this database, you would use the actual sale dates.)

    Creating a series of dates

2. Select A16:A26, and choose the Series command from the Data menu. Excel displays this dialog box:

3. Because the value in cell A16 is a date, Excel assumes you want to create a set of dates. Click the Weekday option, type *4* in the Step Value box, and then click OK. Excel uses the value in cell A16 as its starting point and creates a series of dates that are four days apart, skipping to Monday if a date falls on Saturday or Sunday.

    Calculating dates using Weekdays

4. Select cell A27, highlight 3 in the formula bar, type *7*, and press Enter.

5. Select A27:A37, and choose Repeat Series from the Edit menu.

6. Select cell A38, highlight 3 in the formula bar, type *10*, and press Enter.

7. Select A38:A48, and choose Repeat Series from the Edit menu.

Notice that your worksheet now contains invoices for all four quarters of the year. The formulas in column B have done their work and assigned the invoices to quarters based on the dates in column A.

This large worksheet is ideal for demonstrating some of Excel's database features, but before we launch into that topic, we'll show you how to make INV_LOG.XLS into a template that you can use as a basis for several worksheets.

Creating Templates

Worksheet ideas

Invoice logs like the one you just created can be used as the basis for many kinds of worksheets. For example, you might want to analyze sales by quarter to detect seasonal trends, sales by regional office to determine management effectiveness, and sales by person to evaluate individual performance. If you include product information in your log, you can also evaluate product performance and the contribution of each product to the company's bottom line. To perform any of these analyses, you use a copy of the invoice log, not the log itself, because you want the original log to remain intact as a permanent record.

Excel allows you to designate worksheets as templates that you can use over and over again. When you select a template as the worksheet you want to open, Excel opens a copy of the template, not the template itself, using the template name followed by a number as the worksheet name.

Let's save INVOICES.XLS as a template now. Here's how:

Saving a template

1. Choose Save As from the File menu, and click the Options button. Excel displays this dialog box:

2. Click the arrow at the right end of the File Format drop-down list to display a list of the formats in which you can save a worksheet.

3. Select Template, and click OK to close the Options dialog box.

4. When you return to the Save As dialog box, notice that Excel has changed the extension in the Save Worksheet As text box from XLS to XLT. Click OK to save the template with the name INV_LOG.XLT.

5. Now choose Close from the File menu to close the template.

6. Pull down the File menu, and choose INV_LOG.XLT from the bottom of the menu. Excel opens a copy of the template with the name Inv_Log1, as shown here:

Opening a copy of a template

	Microsoft Excel - Inv_Log1					
File	Edit	Formula	Format	Data	Options	Macro	Window	Help

Normal

	A	B	C	D	E	F	G
1			Invoice Log				
2			*1991*				
3							
4	Date	Quarter	Invoice Number	Salesperson	Office	Amount of Sale	
5	3/9/92	1	4739AA	Crux, Jamie	East	$83,456.23	
6	1/4/92	1	943200	Olderon, Sam	West	$90,875.56	
7	1/10/92	1	8488AA	Karnov, Peter	East	$63,456.83	
8	1/16/92	1	4398AA	Swelden, Chaz	East	$42,356.07	
9	2/3/92	1	4945AA	Crux, Tad	East	$65,643.90	
10	2/8/92	1	825600	Furban, Wally	West	$123,456.45	
11	2/14/92	1	846500	Ladder, Larry	West	$67,345.23	
12	3/2/92	1	4409AA	Karnov, Peter	East	$145,768.34	
13	3/12/92	1	8867AA	Crux, Jamie	East	$43,256.23	
14	3/23/92	1	875600	Ladder, Larry	West	$11,256.90	
15	3/30/92	1	479300	Furban, Wally	West	$85,345.00	
16	4/9/92	2	4739AA	Crux, Jamie	East	$83,456.23	
17	4/15/92	2	943200	Olderon, Sam	West	$90,875.56	
18	4/21/92	2	8488AA	Karnov, Peter	East	$63,456.83	
19	4/27/92	2	4398AA	Swelden, Chaz	East	$42,356.07	

Ready

7. Choose Save from the File menu. Excel then suggests that you save the copy of the template with the name INV_LOG1.XLS. Press Enter to accept this name.

Sorting Data

The sales data in the worksheet you created in Chapter 2 fits neatly on one screen. To find out which salesperson from the West office has made the highest single sale, you could simply look at the worksheet. Getting that information from the worksheet now on your screen is a little more difficult. Fortunately, Excel can quickly sort worksheets like this one, using one, two, or even three levels of sorting.

Adding Sort Codes

Before you sort any large worksheet, you should ask yourself whether you might need to put the data back in its original order. If there is even a chance that you will, you should add sort codes to the worksheet before you begin sorting. A sort code is a sequential number assigned to each row of entries. After sorting the entries, you can sort one more time on the basis of the sort code to put everything back where it was. Follow these steps to add sort codes to INV_LOG1.XLS:

Creating a series of numbers

1. Insert a blank column in front of the Date column by clicking the column A header and choosing Insert from the Edit menu.

2. Select cell A4, type *Sort Code*, and press Enter.

3. In cell A5, type *1*, and press Enter.

4. Select A5:A48, and choose Series from the Data menu.

5. The default settings—Columns as the Series In option, Linear as the Type option, and a Step Value of 1—will produce the result you want, so click OK. Excel uses the value in cell A5 as its starting point and inserts a sequential set of numbers in the selected range, as shown here:

	A	B	C	D	E	F	G
1				Invoice Log			
2				*1991*			
3							
4	Sort Code	Date	Quarter	Invoice Number	Salesperson	Office	Amount of S
5	1	3/9/92	1	4739AA	Crux, Jamie	East	$83,456
6	2	1/4/92	1	943200	Olderon, Sam	West	$90,875
7	3	1/10/92	1	8488AA	Karnov, Peter	East	$63,456
8	4	1/16/92	1	4398AA	Swelden, Chaz	East	$42,356
9	5	2/3/92	1	4945AA	Crux, Tad	East	$65,643
10	6	2/8/92	1	825600	Furban, Wally	West	$123,456
11	7	2/14/92	1	846500	Ladder, Larry	West	$67,345
12	8	3/2/92	1	4409AA	Karnov, Peter	East	$145,768
13	9	3/12/92	1	8867AA	Crux, Jamie	East	$43,256
14	10	3/23/92	1	875600	Ladder, Larry	West	$11,256
15	11	3/30/92	1	479300	Furban, Wally	West	$85,345
16	12	4/9/92	2	4739AA	Crux, Jamie	East	$83,456
17	13	4/15/92	2	943200	Olderon, Sam	West	$90,875
18	14	4/21/92	2	8488AA	Karnov, Peter	East	$63,456
19	15	4/27/92	2	4398AA	Swelden, Chaz	East	$42,356

Now let's look at various ways you might want to sort the INV_LOG1.XLS worksheet.

Using One Sort Key

The simplest sorting procedure is based on only one column, or *sort key*. You indicate which column Excel should use, and the program rearranges the rows of the selected range accordingly. Let's start by sorting the data in INV_LOG1.XLS by regional office so that you can see how the process works:

1. Select A5:G48, and choose Sort from the Data menu. Excel displays this dialog box:

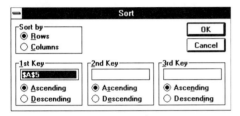

2. In the 1st Key text box, you need to designate the column you want Excel to use as the basis for the sort. Move the dialog box out of the way by dragging its title bar, and click any cell in column F. That cell's absolute reference replaces $A$5 (the active cell of the selected range) in the 1st Key text box.

3. Leave the Sort By option set to Rows and the sort order set to Ascending, and click OK. Turn the page to see the result.

Don't include headings	Sorting by columns	Ascending vs. descending
If you include row 4 in the range to be sorted, Excel sorts the column headings along with the entries. As a result, the headings might end up in the middle of the worksheet. ♦	If your worksheet has headings down the leftmost column instead of across the top row and your data is oriented horizontally instead of vertically, you will want to sort by columns instead of rows. ♦	Ascending order places numbers before text, 1 before 2, and A before B. Descending order, on the other hand, does just the opposite, placing text before numbers, B before A, and 2 before 1. ♦

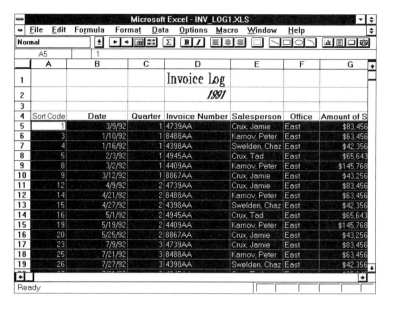

The invoice data is now sorted alphabetically by regional office, with all the invoices for the East office coming before those for the West office. As you can see if you look at the sort codes in column A, within the sorted regions the rows have stayed in numeric order.

Using Two Sort Keys

Now let's take things a step further and sort the invoices not only by regional office but also by salesperson.

1. With A5:G48 selected, choose Sort from the Data menu.

Saving while sorting

Remember to save your worksheet often, perhaps after each sort. You can use Save As to create a new worksheet if you don't want to overwrite the results of one sort with the next. If you have activated the Autosave add-in macro, Excel saves changes automatically at timed intervals that you set. See the documentation for more about add-in macros. ♦

Sort-key default

Excel does not retain sort-key settings from one sort to the next. When you choose the Sort command, the 1st Key text box reflects the active cell of the selected range. You must select the sort keys for every sort. ♦

More than three keys

To sort a range on more than three fields, do multiple sorts. For example, to sort on five fields, first sort with the fifth, or least important, field in the 2nd Key text box and the fourth field in the 1st Key text box. Then sort with the third field in the 3rd Key text box, the second field in the 2nd Key text box, and the most important field in the 1st Key text box. ♦

2. When Excel displays the Sort dialog box, again select
    a cell in column F for the 1st Key. Then click the 2nd
    Key text box, select a cell in column E, and click OK.

The table is now sorted alphabetically by regional office
and alphabetically within region by salesperson.

Using Three Sort Keys

Depending on the focus of your current analysis, you might
want to sort INV_LOG1.XLS based on the Date or Quarter
columns. However, let's assume you are interested in each
person's sales volume and add one more key criteria to the
sort. To sort by regional office, salesperson, and amount of
sale, follow these steps:

1. With the same range still selected, choose Sort from
    the Data menu.
2. Select a cell in column F for the 1st Key, and select a
    cell in column E for the 2nd Key. Then click the 3rd
    Key text box, select a cell in column G, and click OK.

Now you can easily spot the highest sales of each salesperson
in both regions:

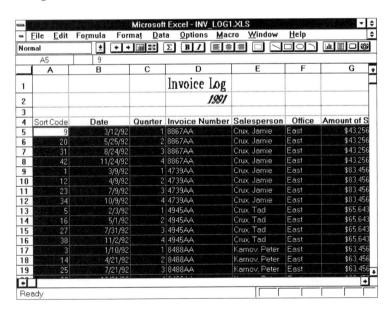

Freezing Headings

As you scroll through the invoice log to check how Excel
has sorted the data, you'll probably find yourself wishing

that the column headings hadn't scrolled out of sight. You can freeze the headings at the top of the screen by splitting the document window into two panes: one containing the headings and the other containing the data. Here's how to split the INV_LOG2.XLS window horizontally:

1. Scroll the worksheet so that row 4—the row with the column headings—is at the top of your screen.
2. Move the mouse pointer to the black bar, called the split bar, at the top of the right scroll bar.

Splitting windows into panes

Split bar

When the pointer changes into a set of arrows, drag the split bar down so that it sits between rows 4 and 5. Here's the result so far:

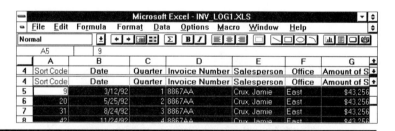

Synchronized scrolling

If you split the worksheet window horizontally and use the bottom scroll bar to scroll the window, both panes of the window scroll so that columns always align. Likewise, if you split the window vertically, using the right scroll bar scrolls the rows simultaneously. ♦

The Split command

The Split command on the worksheet's Control menu (which you access by clicking the dash in the top-left corner of the worksheet window) allows you to split the worksheet window both vertically and horizontally at the same time. Choose the command, and click the worksheet at the location where you want the split bars to intersect. ♦

Freezing panes

The Freeze Panes command on the Options menu lets you lock the top, left, or top-left pane of a split window. You can then keep column or row headings in view while you scroll to other portions of the worksheet. The top and left scroll bars are unavailable when panes are frozen. Choose Unfreeze Panes to unfreeze the frozen window panes. ♦

3. Use the scroll bar for the lower window pane to scroll the sorted data, while the column headings remain visible in the upper window pane.

4. When you have finished viewing the data, restore the single pane by dragging the black bar back up to its original position at the top of the right scroll bar.

Closing split panes

Next, we'll cover Excel's database capabilities. To see how easy it is to perform different kinds of manipulations on different versions of a template, let's save INV_LOG1.XLS in its current state and open a new copy of the template for use in the next section:

1. Save and close INV_LOG1.XLS.

2. Choose INV_LOG.XLT from the bottom of the File menu. Excel opens Inv_Log2 on your screen.

3. Save this copy of the template with the suggested name: INV_LOG2.XLS.

Database Basics

The invoice log is an organized collection of information about invoices. By common definition, it is a database.

A database is a table of related data with a rigid structure that enables you to easily locate and evaluate individual items of information. Each row of a database is a record that contains all the pertinent information about one component of the database. For example, row 5 of the invoice log contains all the information about one particular invoice. Each cell of the database is a field that contains one item of information. For example, cell F5 contains the amount of the invoice for the record in row 5. All the fields in a particular column contain the same kind of information about their respective records. For example, column G of the invoice log contains the amounts of all the invoices. At the top of each column is a heading, called the field name.

Although the invoice log is a database by common definition, Excel does not yet recognize it as a database. Here's how you tell Excel that the log is a database:

1. Select A4:F49.

2. Choose Set Database from the Data menu.

Setting a database

That's it. After you specifically designate the range A4:F49 as a database, you can use commands on the Data menu to pull records that meet specific criteria out of the database for further examination or manipulation.

Manipulating Records

Database ideas

Suppose you invested a considerable chunk of your advertising budget for the year on a direct-mail flyer about a two-week promotion. For another two-week promotion earlier in the year, you relied on your salespeople to get the word out to their customers. You want to compare sales during the two promotions. Or suppose you want to analyze all sales over $60,000 to see if you can detect sales patterns. In either case, you can tell Excel to extract all the relevant invoices for scrutiny.

You give Excel instructions of this kind by defining criteria in an area of the worksheet called the criteria range. For example, you might tell Excel to find all the records with amounts over $60,000 by entering *<60000* in the criteria range under the Amount of Sale field name.

Creating the Criteria Range

As with worksheet calculation areas, it's a good idea to locate the criteria range at the top of the worksheet so that it is easy to jump to from anywhere in the database. Let's insert a block

---

Field-naming conventions

Excel has several distinct rules concerning field names in databases. No two field names can be the same. Also, field names cannot begin with a numeric value and cannot be blank. If they are, Excel will display an error message during database operations. ♦

Mandatory field names

You must include the field names in the database range. If you neglect to include them, Excel will be unable to perform the Extract, Find, or Delete commands. ♦

Only one database

Although you can build several tables of information on the same worksheet, only one of them can be designated as the active database at any given time. When you choose Set Database, Excel assigns the name Database to the selected range. Setting a different database assigns the name Database to the newly selected range. ♦

of four rows above the database field names to use as a criteria range.

1. Select the headers for rows 4 through 7.

2. Choose Insert from the Edit menu. Excel inserts the number of rows you selected.

The top row of the criteria range always contains the field names of the fields you want to use as criteria for locating records, so start by copying the field names from the database to the criteria range:

1. Select A8:F8, and choose Copy from the Edit menu.

2. Select A4, and choose the Paste command from the Edit menu. Here's the result:

Now you need to set the criteria range so that Excel knows where in the database to look for the criteria. Follow the steps on the next page.

Adding records

When setting the database, always include at least one blank row at the bottom of the selected range. Then if you need to add records to the database, you can simply select the blank row and insert a new row to extend the database, instead of having to redefine the database. ◆

Data forms

After you have set the database, you can use the Form command on the Data menu to create, find, view, edit, and delete records. When you choose Form, Excel opens a dialog box with the first record of the database displayed. Field names are shown in text boxes on the left side of the dialog box, and the records are displayed on the left side . You can edit any field except those derived from formulas, such as the Quarter and Office fields in the example above. Use the scroll bar to scroll through the records, and click the buttons in the dialog box to delete, create, and find records. ◆

*Setting the
criteria range*

1. Select A4:F5, a range that includes the field names and the blank row beneath them where you will enter your criteria.
2. Choose Set Criteria from the Data menu.

Entering Criteria

To have Excel locate specific records, you enter one or more criteria under the field names in the criteria range. For example, to locate all the invoices for Peter Karnov, you simply enter *Karnov, Peter* under the Salesperson field name in the criteria range. To locate invoices that are both for Peter Karnov *and* have amounts over $100,000—Excel is to locate records that meet both criteria—you enter *Karnov, Peter* under Salesperson, and *>100000* in the same row under Amount of Sale. To locate the invoices for Peter Karnov *or* Wally Furban—Excel is to locate records that meet either of the two criteria—you enter *Karnov, Peter* under the Salesperson field name in the first row and *Furban, Wally* under the Salesperson field name in the next row. (You then need to reset the criteria range to include the second row.)

Let's try entering criteria that will locate invoices for Peter Karnov that amount to more than $100,000:

1. In cell D5, type *Karnov, Peter*.
2. In cell F5, type *>100000*.

Using all field names	**Only one criteria range**	**No blank rows**
Technically, you can enter only the names of the fields you use as criteria in the criteria range. However, copying all the field names into your criteria range allows you to mix and match criteria as necessary, without having to erase and type field names each time. ♦	Only one range can be designated as the criteria range at any given time. When you choose Set Criteria, Excel assigns the name Criteria to the selected range. Setting a different criteria range assigns the name Criteria to the newly selected range. ♦	Never include blank rows in the criteria range. If you do, Excel selects all the records, because the blank row does not specify any particular criteria. The presence of blank rows in the criteria range is particularly dangerous when you use the Delete command, because all records will be deleted. ♦

You must now choose a command from the Data menu to tell Excel what to do with the records that match the criteria. Three commands are available: Find, Delete, and Extract.

Finding and Deleting Records

Choosing Find from the Data menu tells Excel to find and highlight the first record in the database that meets the criteria you entered in the criteria range. Let's try this now:

1. Choose Find from the Data menu. Excel stops at this record:

Finding records

2. Click the arrows at the bottom and top of the right scroll bar to move to the next and previous records that meet the criteria. (You can also press the Down and Up Arrow keys.)

3. Choose the Exit Find command from the Data menu to leave find mode or press Esc.

Leaving find mode

Comparison operators

You can use these comparison operators to compute criteria:

= > < >= <= <>

and you can specify wildcards, using the standard DOS wildcards * and ? for matching text. ◆

Criteria in same field

If you want to locate records using two criteria in the same field, you must add a second field with the same field name to the criteria range. For example, to locate invoices that are dated after June 30 and before July 15, you would add a second Date field name, either in cell G4 or adjacent to the existing

Date field name in cell A4, reset the criteria range, and enter *>6/30/91* under one Date field name and *<7/15/91* under the other Date field name. ◆

Deleting records →

Choosing Delete from the Data menu tells Excel to find and delete the records that meet the criteria in the criteria range. When you choose this command, Excel displays a message box to warn you that the matching records will be permanently deleted. Click OK to proceed with the deletion, or click Cancel if you first want to check that the criteria you have entered won't cause Excel to delete records you really need to keep.

Extracting Records

Choosing Extract from the Data menu tells Excel to find and copy the records that meet the criteria into an area of the worksheet called the extract range. Before choosing this command, you must set the extract range so that Excel knows where to put the records. The procedure for creating the extract range is almost identical to the procedure for creating the criteria range, except that we always locate the extract range to the right of all existing worksheet entries so that there is no chance that extracted records will overwrite valuable information. Follow these steps to create an extract range in INV_LOG2.XLS:

1. Select A8:F8 (the field-name cells), and choose Copy from the Edit menu.
2. Select H4, and choose Paste from the Edit menu.
3. To widen the columns to fit the headings, choose Column Width from the Format menu, and click the

---

Extract range field names

As with the criteria range, the top row of the extract range must contain field names. If you include only some of the fields, Excel extracts only those fields from the database. ♦

Extracting unique records

The Unique Records Only option in the Extract dialog box allows you to tell Excel to extract only one instance of repeated records. Because we repeated many records to create our database, selecting this option would result in fewer records in our extract range. ♦

Preserving extracted records

When you extract records, Excel overwrites any previously extracted records. If you want to preserve the records, you must move either the records or the extract range. ♦

Best Fit button. Then widen the Date column slightly so that the dates will fit.

4. To allocate space for the extracted records, select H4:M4, and choose Set Extract from the Data menu. You can include cells below the field names in the extract range, but selecting a range limits the number of records Excel can extract to the size of the range.

Setting the extract range

Now you can tell Excel to extract the records that meet the criteria in the criteria range:

1. Choose Extract from the Data menu. Excel displays this dialog box:

```
┌─────────────────────────────────────────┐
│  Extract                ┌──────────┐     │
│                         │    OK    │     │
│   ☐ Unique Records Only └──────────┘     │
│                         ┌──────────┐     │
│                         │  Cancel  │     │
│                         └──────────┘     │
└─────────────────────────────────────────┘
```

2. Click OK to start the extraction. Here's the result:

H	I	J	K	L	M	N	O
Date	Quarter	Invoice Number	Salesperson	Office	Amount of Sale		
3/2/92	1	4409AA	Karnov, Peter	East	$145,768.34		
5/19/92	2	4409AA	Karnov, Peter	East	$145,768.34		
8/18/92	3	4409AA	Karnov, Peter	East	$145,768.34		
11/18/92	4	4409AA	Karnov, Peter	East	$145,768.34		

This discussion of databases has necessarily been brief, but you should now know enough to explore ways of manipulating your own data using criteria and the Data-menu commands. For now, let's get ready for the next section by loading a new copy of INV_LOG.XLT:

1. Save and close INV_LOG2.XLS.

2. Choose INV_LOG.XLT from the bottom of the File menu, and save the worksheet that appears with the name INV_LOG3.XLS.

Consolidating Data

An important new feature of Excel 3 is the ability to extract totals from sets of data like the sample invoice log, without having to perform multiple sorting operations and multiple SUM functions. Called consolidation, this feature enables Excel to perform several functions on part of the data in a worksheet, based either on a name associated with the data or on its position. Sound confusing? An example will not only clarify the concept of consolidation, but will also give you some ideas about how to make use of it. Let's do a couple of consolidations using INV_LOG3.XLS. First, we'll add the sales amounts by regional office, locating the result of the consolidation at the bottom of the database:

Setting the consolidate range

1. Select cell A50 as the top-left corner of the range that Excel will use to report the results of the consolidation.

2. Choose Consolidate from the Data menu. Excel displays this dialog box:

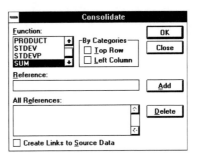

3. The Function list box displays the functions that you can use when consolidating. Leave the default selection, SUM, highlighted.

4. In the By Categories section of the dialog box, select the Left Column option, and check that the Top Row option is not selected. The Left Column option tells Excel to consolidate the information based on the left column of the range referenced in the Reference text box.

5. Click the Reference text box, and type *E5:F48* (the Office and Amount of Sale columns). You could also drag the dialog box out of the way and select the range with the mouse.

6. Click OK. Excel totals the sales amounts for each regional office and puts the results in cells B50:B51, with the East and West labels appearing to the left of them in A50:A51. (Adjust the column widths as necessary to see the totals.)

Now let's consolidate the amounts by salesperson:

1. First, select cell C50 as the top-left corner of the consolidate range.
2. Next, choose Consolidate from the Data menu.
3. Leave the Function and By Categories options just as they are.
4. In the All References list box, select the previous range consolidated, and click the Delete button.
5. Click the Reference text box, type *D5:F48*, and click OK. Excel lists the salespeople's names in column C and their total sales in column E. Excel leaves column D blank because it can't consolidate the information in the Office column.
6. To move the totals to column D, select them, choose Cut from the Edit menu, select cell D50, and then choose Paste.

Consolidating discontiguous ranges

Finally, let's total the amounts by quarter:

1. Select cell E50, and then choose Consolidate from the Data menu.
2. Leave the Function and By Categories options just as they are.

Room for consolidation

When you designate a cell as the top-left corner of the consolidate range, be sure that there is plenty of room below the range for the consolidated information, because Excel overwrites any existing information. In the first example, you know that consolidating by region will require only two rows: one for East and one for West. But in the second example, if you are unsure how many rows consolidating by salesperson will require, be certain that only blank cells are below the consolidate range. ♦

Inadvertent consolidation

If you do not delete the range used in the previous consolidation from the All References list box, Excel will consolidate the previous range with any new range you add to the list. ♦

3. In the All References list box, select the previous range consolidated, and click the Delete button.

4. Click the Reference text box, type B5:F48, and click OK. Excel lists the four quarters in column E and the consolidated amounts in column I, again leaving blank columns for the intervening data.

5. To move the totals to column F, select I50:I53, choose Cut from the Edit menu, select cell F50, and then choose Paste. Here's the result of the consolidations:

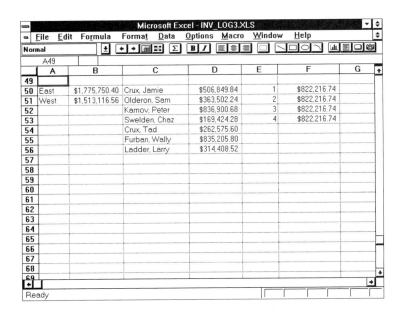

Consolidation by position

In our example, we consolidate by name; that is, we use the category name to consolidate values. If you are working with several worksheets with similar information in the exact same cells, you can consolidate the information by position. Leave the By Categories options deselected and don't select the category labels when adding cell ranges to the All References list box. ◆

Adding consolidation ranges

Using the Add button in the Consolidate dialog box, you can select several different ranges on different worksheets from which you want Excel to consolidate information. Select the ranges, and then click the Add button to add them to the list in the All References list box. If you make a mistake, highlight the range in the All References list box, and then click the Delete button. Click OK when you have finished adding ranges. Excel will then consolidate the information from the designated worksheets into the consolidate range on the active worksheet. ◆

Now let's total the amounts for the salespeople to get a grand total:

1. Select D57.
2. Click the Auto-sum tool on the Toolbar, click the Enter box, and format the result as currency. Excel displays the result, $3,288,866.96, in cell D57.

We'll use the consolidated totals later in this chapter, after we have created a couple of worksheets that we can link to INV_LOG3.XLS. To create these worksheets, let's take a detour and learn about another new feature of Excel 3: workgroups.

Using Workgroups

Suppose you want to use the information in INV_LOG3.XLS to analyze the performance of your salespeople. You want to create identical worksheets for each person—that's seven worksheets to set up before you can get going with the analysis. In this section, we'll demonstrate how you can use workgroups to reduce that set-up time.

Workgroups are worksheets that you temporarily link together so that any editing or formatting that you do in one is applied to the others. Let's take a closer look. To make it easier for you to follow along, we'll create just two new worksheets, but you can create as many as you need.

1. Create two new worksheets, by choosing the New command from the File menu, selecting Worksheet in the New dialog box, and clicking OK for each one.
2. With one of the new worksheets active, choose Save As from the File menu, and then save the file as REV_WFUR.XLS.
3. Choose the other new worksheet from the Window menu, and save it as REV_PKAR.XLS.
4. Choose Workgroup from the Window menu. Excel displays this dialog box:

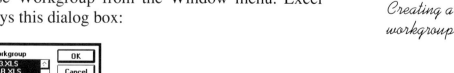

Creating a workgroup

Excel assumes that you want all open worksheets to be in the workgroup and highlights their names in the dialog box.

Designating group members

5. You want only the new worksheets in the workgroup, so deselect INV_LOG3.XLS by holding down the Shift key and clicking its name in the list. Then click OK.

6. So that you can see both workgroup worksheets at the same time, choose Arrange Workgroup from the Window menu. Your screen now looks like this:

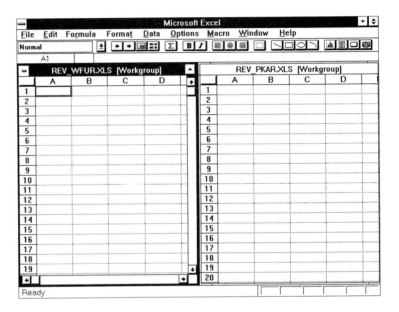

As you can see, Excel arranges the two workgroup worksheets so that they take up half the screen each. Notice that [Workgroup] appears next to the names in the worksheet title bars to remind you that you are working in a workgroup.

The worksheet that was active when you chose the Workgroup command—REV_PKAR.XLS, in this case—becomes the workgroup "leader." Changes you make to this worksheet are reflected in all other workgroup worksheets. If you activate any other worksheet, Excel disbands the workgroup.

Disbanding a workgroup

Entering and Formatting Text

Let's start by entering a few labels so that the information in these worksheets is easy to understand at a glance:

1. Make the following entries in the active worksheet:

A1	SALES PERFORMANCE, 1991
A3	Name
A4	Base Salary
A5	Commission Rate (%)
A6	Commission
A7	Your Sales
A8	Region's Sales
A9	Total Sales
A10	Sales Expense (%)
A11	Contribution to Region's Sales (%)
A12	Contribution to Total Sales (%)

2. Select A1:A12, and click the Bold tool.

3. Widen column A until all the entries are visible. All the entries and formatting you made in the first worksheet appear in the second, as shown here:

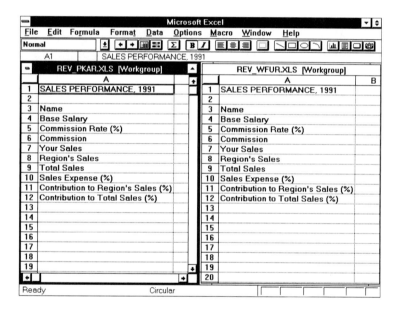

Entering Formulas

Now it's time to get to the heart of the matter. While still in the workgroup, we'll enter some base data and then add the necessary formulas.

1. So that you have some room to work in, maximize REV_PKAR.XLS by clicking the Maximize button (the up arrowhead) in the window's top-right corner.

2. Enter the following values in the indicated cells:

B3   Peter Karnov
B4 $18,000
B5   2%
B6   =B5*B7
B10   =(B4+B6)/B7
B11   =B7/B8
B12   =B7/B9

Excel displays a #DIV/0 error message in cells B10:B12 to indicate that the formulas in those cells have a divisor of zero. The error will disappear when you enter values in cells B7:B9.

3. You entered the base salary and the commission rate "in format," as currency and a percentage. As their labels indicate, cells B6:B9 also need to be formatted as currency, so select them, and then select Currency from the Style drop-down list box on the Toolbar. B10:B12 need to be formatted as percentages, so select them, and then select Percent from the Style list box.

4. Click the Restore button (the double-headed arrow) in the menu bar to redisplay the two worksheets side-by-side.

Saving workgroup worksheets

5. Before we go any further, let's save the worksheets. Choose Save from the File menu. Because the workgroup is still active, all the workgroup worksheets are saved. Here's the result so far:

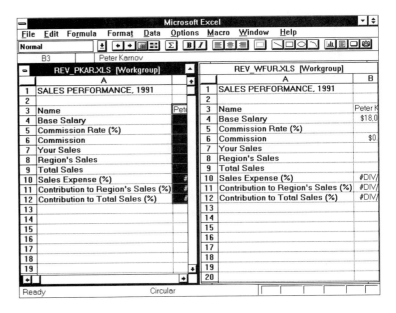

Linking Worksheets

The values you need to enter in cells B6:B8 are available in INV_LOG3.XLS, but unfortunately, to reference this data you need to make INV_LOG3.XLS the active worksheet, which will dissolve the workgroup. So let's finish these worksheets one by one, linking them to INV_LOG3.XLS as we go.

1. Click anywhere in REV_WFUR.XLS to break up the workgroup. Notice that [Workgroup] has disappeared from the title bars of both worksheets.

2. Select B7, type =, choose INV_LOG3.XLS from the Window menu, and click Peter Karnov's sales amount in cell D52. Then click the Enter box.

3. Now select B8 of REV_PKAR.XLS, type =, choose INV_LOG3.XLS from the Window menu, and then click East's sales amount in cell B50. Next, click the Enter box.

4. Select B9, type =, choose INV_LOG3.XLS from the Window menu, and click the total sales amount in cell D57. Then click the Enter box. Expand the window to full size and adjust column B's width. The #DIV/0 errors have been replaced by the formula results, as shown on the following page.

Common error messages

When Excel can't understand what you are attempting to do in a cell, it displays an error value in that cell. #DIV/0! is a common error value, indicating that you are attempting to divide by zero. The #N/A error indicates that the formula in the current cells refers to a cell that doesn't contain any information. The #NAME? error value indicates that you have used a name in a formula that Excel can't find in the Define Name dialog box. The #NUM! error value tells you that Excel has found an erroneous argument in a formula requiring a number. The #VALUE! error means that you have created a formula that attempts to perform a mathematical operation with a text value. The #REF! error indicates that you have deleted a cell or range that was included in a formula. ♦

Returning to a workgroup

Excel remembers which worksheets were part of your last workgroup. If you disband the workgroup by selecting another worksheet, you can return to the workgroup by choosing Workgroup from the Window menu and clicking OK. ♦

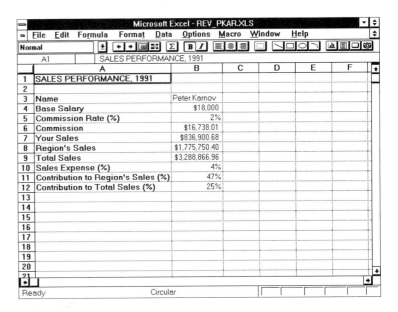

5. Now choose REV_WFUR.XLS from the bottom of the
    Window menu, change the name in cell B3, and adjust
    the base salary and commission rate in B4 and B5 to
    $19,500 and 3% respectively.

6. Repeat steps 2, 3, and 4, clicking cell D55 to enter
    Wally Furban's sales amount in step 2, and clicking
    B51 to enter West's sales amount in step 3.

You've just learned how to link worksheets. By creating
simple formulas in REV_PKAR.XLS and REV_WFUR.XLS
that reference cells in INV_LOG3.XLS, you have linked the
two performance-review worksheets to the invoice log. Now

XLSTART directory

When you first installed
Excel, the installation program created a subdirectory
called XLSTART in the Excel
directory. Any worksheet,
chart, macro sheet, or add-in
macro you place in this directory will be opened when
you start Excel. This directory is especially handy if
you frequently use the same
set of macros or a worksheet
template. ◆

Starting where you left off

The Save Workspace com-
mand on the File menu is a
great way to pick up exactly
where you left off during
your last Excel work session.
Suppose you are forced to
quit Excel in the middle of
this session. If you simply
save the work you've done
and quit Excel, you'll have to
open all three worksheets
again when you start the next
session. Choosing the Save

Workspace command dis-
plays a dialog box so that you
can name the current workspace, which includes all the
open worksheets. Usually,
you'll want to accept the default name, RESUME.XLW,
by clicking OK. The next
time you start Excel, you can
open RESUME.XLW to open
all three worksheets at once,
exactly as they were when
you saved the workspace. ◆

if the values in the linked cells in INV_LOG3.XLS change, the results of the linking formulas in REV_PKAR.XLS and REV_WFUR.XLS will also change.

The link is carried out by means of an external reference that enables Excel to quickly find the supporting cell and then pull information from it. Now let's take a look at an external reference:

External references

1. In REV_WFUR.XLS, select cell B9, which contains the total sales amount, and look at the formula bar:

The first part of the reference is the name of the supporting worksheet, INV_LOG3.XLS, followed by an exclamation point (!). The exclamation point is Excel's clue that the reference is outside the current worksheet. Next comes the absolute reference of the cell in INV_LOG3.XLS that contains the total sales amount, $D$57.

2. Now look at the same formula on the REV_PKAR.XLS worksheet.

3. Hold down the Shift key, and choose Close All from the File menu. Excel prompts you to save each work-sheet before it closes each one. Click Yes in each case.

Closing all worksheets

We'll leave you to experiment with the linking formulas you have created. Try making and saving a few changes to the amounts in the invoice log, consolidating the amounts, and then closing the log. When you open the performance-review worksheets, Excel asks whether you want to update references to unopened documents. If you click Yes, Excel reads the new values from the unopened INV_LOG3.XLS and updates the performance-review worksheets accordingly.

Updating linked worksheets

4

Tracking Budgets

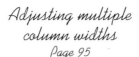

Adjusting multiple
column widths
Page 95

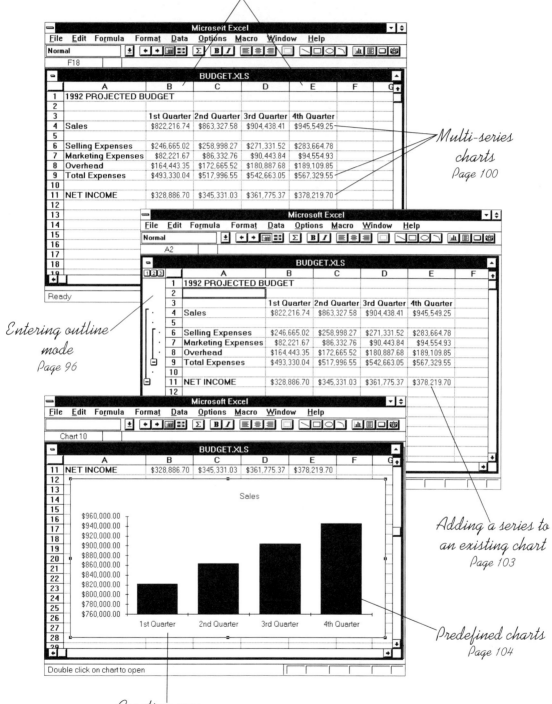

Multi-series
charts
Page 100

Entering outline
mode
Page 96

Adding a series to
an existing chart
Page 103

Predefined charts
Page 104

Creating new
charts
Page 103

In the previous chapters, you learned a lot about Excel, and you now know enough to put Excel to use in your own business environment. After all that hard work, let's relax a bit. Using a budget worksheet as a basis, in this chapter we take a brief look at outlining and then explore the various ways you can visually present worksheet data.

Setting Up the Budget

Before we can get going, we need to set up this projected budget worksheet:

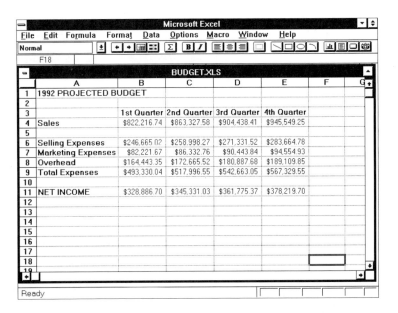

Once the worksheet is in place, we can plot the budget information as various kinds of charts. Assuming that Excel is loaded, follow these steps to create the worksheet:

1. If you do not have a new, blank worksheet on your screen, close any open worksheets, choose New from the File menu, and click OK.
2. Save the worksheet as BUDGET.XLS.
3. In cell A1, type 1992 PROJECTED BUDGET as the worksheet title, click the Enter box, and then make the title bold.
4. In cell B3, type *1st Quarter*, and press Tab to enter the value and select cell C3. Then enter *2nd Quarter*, *3rd*

Quarter, and *4th Quarter* in cells C3:E3. Make these headings bold and centered.

5. Now manually adjust the width of columns B through E so that the headings fit. Instead of selecting one column at a time, select all four columns by clicking the header of column B and dragging through the header of column E. Then adjust the width of one of the columns. All four columns take on the new width.

Adjusting multiple column widths

6. In cell A4, type *Sales*, and click the Enter box. Then make the Sales heading bold.

7. Next, enter these sales amounts in the indicated cells:

    B4   822216.74
    C4   863327.58
    D4   904438.41
    E4   945549.25

Now let's tackle the expenses. For this example, assume that we have selling expenses that average 30 percent of sales, marketing expenses that average 10 percent, and overhead expenses (fixed costs) that average 20 percent.

1. Enter the following information in the indicated cells:

    A6   Selling Expenses
    A7   Marketing Expenses
    A8   Overhead
    A9   Total Expenses
    B6   =.3*B4
    B7   =.1*B4
    B8   =.2*B4
    B9   =SUM(B6:B8)

2. Select B6:E9, and choose Fill Right from the Edit menu to duplicate the 1st quarter formulas for the 2nd, 3rd, and 4th quarters.

3. Select B4:E11, and then select Currency from the Style list box on the Toolbar.

4. Select A6:A11, and click the Bold tool on the Toolbar. Then choose Column Width from the Format menu, and select the Best Fit option.

Finally, let's compute the net income:

1. In cell A11, type *NET INCOME*, and click the Enter box.

2. In cell B11, type an equal sign, click cell B4, type a minus sign (–), click cell B9, and click the Enter box. Excel enters the result, $328,886.70, as the 1st quarter's net income.

3. Use Fill Right to copy the formula in cell B11 to cells C11:E11.

Viola! Your budget worksheet should now look like the one shown earlier.

Outlining Worksheets

Although our sample budget is a very simple one, imagine trying to read a large complex budget with hundreds of entries and many different totals. Excel's outlining feature lets you view as little or as much of a worksheet as you want to see. It searches for what it considers to be the most important information (for example, totals) and uses this information to create different outline row and column levels. When you are in outline mode, you can simply click a button to view the different levels. Let's try the outline feature on our sample worksheet.

Entering outline mode

1. Select cell A2, then click the Outline tool on the Toolbar or choose Outline from the Formula menu, and click OK.

Outline tool

Excel then displays a dialog box telling you that no outline exists in the worksheet and asking whether it should create one. By default, Excel looks to the right and below the selected cell to create the outline. If you want to outline only a portion of the worksheet, select that portion before creating the outline. To tell Excel to look in only one direction to create the outline, select options in the Outline dialog box.

2. Click OK. Excel enters outline mode and displays the row level buttons on the left side of the screen:

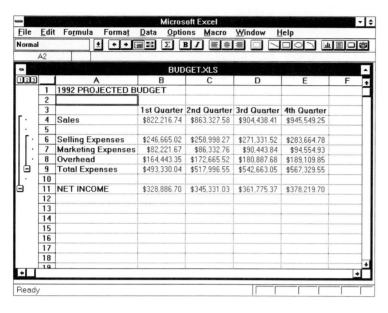

Initially, an outlined worksheet appears fully expanded. The row level buttons indicate the number of outline levels (you can have up to seven). You use the buttons to expand and collapse the outline, as you'll see:

1. Collapse the outline one level by clicking the button labeled 2. Here's the result:

Collapsing one level

Notice that rows 6 through 8 are hidden and that a plus sign appears on the button next to row 9. Excel deduced that row 9 was the "bottom line" of the set of entries in rows 6 through 9 and now displays only row 9.

Expanding the outline

2. Click the button with the plus sign to expand the outline.

3. Click the row level button labeled 1. Excel collapses the outline as far as it can, as shown here:

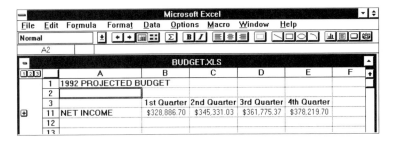

Excel has retained the column headings and the last row of the table, hiding all intervening levels and allowing you to get to the "bottom line."

Although hiding the rows in this worksheet does not produce revolutionary results, you can imagine the potential for manipulating large sections of data. For example, you could collapse a section of a worksheet containing the sum of 900 rows of data. By selecting the outline of the section and choosing the Copy command from the Edit menu, you could then copy all the data. If you pasted the outline in another worksheet, all 900 rows would also be pasted.

Copying collapsed outlines

Leaving outline mode

Here's how you leave outline mode:

1. First, expand the outline fully by clicking the row level button labeled 3 or the button with the plus sign.

2. Next, click the Outline tool on the toolbar.

Selecting visible cells

The Select Visible Cells tool on the Toolbar allows you to select collapsed outlines. For example, you can click the Select Visible Cells tool to select only rows 3 and 11 in the collapsed budget worksheet. Then you can choose Copy from the Edit menu to copy them. If you select the rows manually, Excel also selects all the rows between them. ◆

Changing outline levels

Click the Promote and Demote tools on the Toolbar to raise or lower the outline level of the selected row or column. In the example above, clicking row 11 and then clicking the Demote tool demotes the row from level 1 to level 2. ◆

Another way to hide rows

To hide rows manually, select the row header, and choose Row Height from the Format menu. Click the Hide button to set the row height to 0. To unhide the row, select it by dragging through adjacent row headers or use Goto to activate one of the row's cells. Then choose Row Height, and click Unhide. Hide columns the same way, using Column Width. ◆

Creating Charts in the Worksheet Environment

With Excel 3, you can create charts in two ways: as separate documents or as part of the worksheet. In this section, we show you how to quickly plot data on the worksheet. The advantage of this method is that you can then save and print the chart and the underlying worksheet as one document.

To create worksheet charts, you use the Chart tool on the Toolbar:

Chart tool

1. Select A3:E4, and click the Chart tool.
2. Move the cross-hair pointer to the blank area below your worksheet entries, hold down the mouse button, and drag to create a marquee about the size of the worksheet window. Then release the mouse button. Here's the result:

Drawing the chart frame

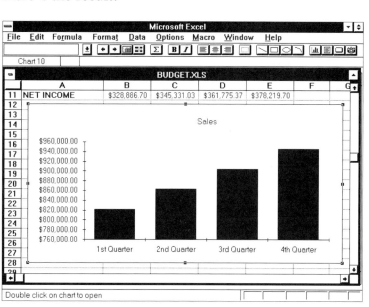

Excel has drawn a column chart of the data in A3:E4, with the 1st, 2nd, 3rd, and 4th Quarter labels along the x-axis (the horizontal axis) and dollar amounts at regular intervals along the y-axis (the vertical axis). The label from cell A4, Sales, has been used as the chart's title.

We have plotted only one set of data, called a data series. Let's see what the chart looks like when we plot two series:

Deleting worksheet charts

1. The single-series chart should be active. (Black squares called handles appear around the chart's perimeter to indicate that it is active.) If it isn't, simply click it.

2. Press the Del key to delete the chart.

Multi-series charts

3. Select A3:E4 again, and then hold down the Ctrl key and select A11:E11. Click the Chart tool, and drag another marquee in the blank area below the worksheet entries. Excel draws this chart comparing total sales and net income for each quarter:

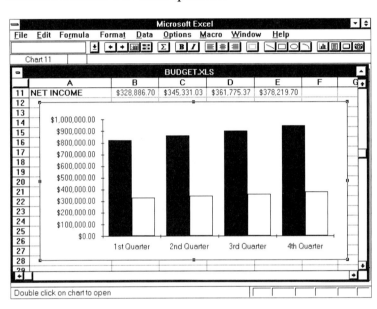

Headings as labels

If you include the column or row headings when selecting the data you want Excel to chart, Excel uses the headings as axis labels, whether you are creating a worksheet chart or an independent chart document. ♦

Moving and sizing

You can move a worksheet chart anywhere on the screen by dragging it. You can make it larger or smaller by dragging one of the black squares around its frame in the direction in which you want the frame to grow. ♦

Preferred format

By default, Excel creates worksheet charts in what's called the Preferred format. When you first start Excel, the Preferred format is a plain column chart. See page 107 for information about how to change the Preferred format. ♦

The new chart has no title because Excel does not know which of the two labels, Sales or Net Income, to use. The sales amounts and net-income amounts are grouped in quarters and are represented by columns of different colors (or shades). A legend would help us identify which is which, but we cannot add a legend directly to a worksheet chart. To add a legend and otherwise format this chart, we need to open it as a separate document in Excel's chart environment (see page 108).

Worksheet charts are actively linked to the data Excel uses to plot them, and they automatically change if the data changes. Try this:

Automatic updating

1. Change one of the net income figures. The net-income column grows or shrinks to reflect the change.
2. Choose Undo Entry from the Edit menu to undo the changes.

Making Worksheet Charts Independent

As you have just seen, creating worksheet charts is very easy. You simply select the data, click the chart tool, and create the chart frame. Excel fills in all the details. If you want to format this chart or change it to a different type (see page 104 for more about chart types), you need to open the chart in the chart environment. Let's do that now by following the steps on the next page.

Chart scale	Source format	Underlying values
If you change the source data radically, the scale of the entire chart may change. For example, if you enter a sales amount in the millions in BUDGET.XLS, the other columns will shrink down to almost nothing to keep the scale consistent. ◆	If you change the format of the source data—for example, if you select B4:E11 in BUDGET.XLS, choose Number from the Format menu, and then select currency with no cents ($#,##0)—the labels along the y-axis change accordingly. ◆	The format of the values does not affect the way they are plotted. Excel always uses the underlying values when plotting charts. ◆

1. Double-click anywhere inside the chart frame. The chart now appears inside a window with the name of the worksheet followed by the word Chart and a number in its title bar:

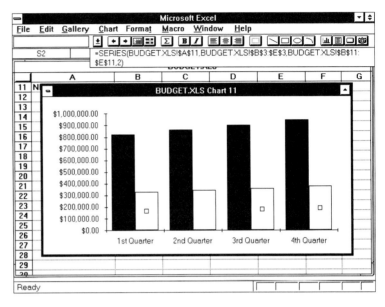

2. Move the window to one side by dragging its title bar. As you can see, the original worksheet chart still resides on the worksheet. You are, in effect, working with a copy of the chart.

3. Click the Maximize button in the window's top-right corner. Excel enlarges the chart window to fill the entire screen.

4. Save this chart by choosing Save As from the File menu, typing *budget1*, and clicking OK. Excel identifies the file as a chart document by adding the extension XLC to the filename.

5. Close the chart window by choosing Close from the File menu.

Creating Charts in the Chart Environment

The traditional method of creating a chart in Excel is to copy the data directly to the chart environment and then format the chart there. You move to the chart environment from the

worksheet environment simply by opening a chart document. The chart environment differs from the worksheet
environment in several respects, as you'll see in a minute.

When you create a chart in the chart environment, the
worksheet containing the source data and the chart are separate files that you can save and print independently. However, the chart and its source data are still linked, and Excel
updates the chart to reflect changes in the data. Let's experiment, again using the budget worksheet:

1. Select A3:E4, and choose New from the File menu.
   Excel displays the New dialog box.

2. Select Chart, and click OK to create a new chart document. Excel uses the data in the selected range to plot
   a chart that is virtually identical to the first worksheet
   chart you created:

Creating new charts

To create a two-series chart identical to BUDGET1.XLC,
you could start all over, but there is an easier way:

1. Make BUDGET.XLS active, select A11:E11, and then
   choose Copy from the Edit menu.

2. Make the new chart active, and choose Paste from the
   Edit menu. Excel pastes in the second data series.
   Using this technique, you can create charts piecemeal
   from many different sources.

Adding a series to an existing chart

3. Excel assigns the names Chart1, Chart2, and so on to newly created charts. Change this name now by choosing Save As from the File menu, typing *budget2*, and clicking OK.

Now take a look at the chart environment. All the tools on the Toolbar except Bold and Italic are inactive. The menu bar no longer has a Formula, Data, or Options menu, but it has gained a Gallery and Chart menu. If you pull down the Format menu, you'll see that its commands have changed significantly so that you can format charts to look their best.

No matter what kind of chart you need—column, bar, pie, line, and so on—Excel has a format that will do the job. But we have found that we rarely need really flashy charts, such as 3-D charts. Usually, we can come up with impressive visual support for our worksheets by carefully selecting from among Excel's many predefined chart types. We take a look at these next.

Changing the Chart Type

Predefined charts

Excel organizes its built-in chart types into galleries that you can access from the Gallery menu. The available types include:

- Column charts (the default type), which are ideal for showing the variations in the value of an item over time, as with the budget example.

The SERIES function

If you click one of the columns in the chart document, a SERIES function appears in the formula bar. This function links the chart to the source worksheet. Notice that the external references are all absolute. If you change the position of linked data, the chart has no way of finding the moved data. ♦

Updating linked data

Each time you open a chart document without opening the linked worksheet that contains the chart data, Excel displays the message *Update references to unopened documents?* When you click the Yes button, Excel looks at the unopened worksheet to see if the data has changed, and if so, changes the chart accordingly. ♦

Big charts

The chart in an independent chart document can be only as large as the screen. You can make a worksheet chart as big as a billboard if you want, because you can scroll the chart frame beyond the edge of the screen. Practical uses of this undocumented feature might be limited, but it's fun to play with! ♦

- Bar charts, which are great for showing the values of several items at a single point in time. (The "columns" representing the values are rotated 90 degrees so that they are horizontal.)
- Line charts, which are often used to show variations in the value of more than one item over time.
- Area charts, which look something like line charts but which plot multiple data series as cumulative layers with different colors, patterns, or shades.
- Pie charts, which are ideal for showing the percentages of an item that can be assigned to the item's components. (Pie charts can plot only one data series.)
- Scatter diagrams, which are used to detect correlations between independent items (such as a person's height and weight).
- 3-D charts, which add a third dimension to column, line, area, and pie charts.

In addition, you can create various kinds of combination charts, which plot one type of chart on top of another as an "overlay."

Each gallery offers several variations that will satisfy most of your charting needs. Let's try changing the type of the chart currently on your screen so that you can see some of the possibilities.

1. Choose Bar from the Gallery menu, select format 6, and click OK.

Creating bar charts

Chart conversion

Just as you can convert a worksheet chart into an independent chart document, after creating a chart in the chart environment you can easily paste it into an Excel worksheet as a worksheet chart. First choose Select Chart from the Chart menu, and then choose Copy from the Edit menu. Select the worksheet, and choose Paste from the Edit menu. The chart appears in the worksheet, where you can move or size it as needed. ♦

Combining for contrast

When you want to contrast two or more series or emphasize a significant relationship, try plotting your data as a combination chart. Combination charts consist of a main chart of one type and an overlay chart of another type. A common combination is a main column chart and a line overlay chart. ♦

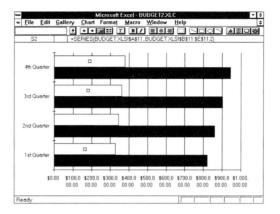

Creating line charts

2. Choose Line from the Gallery menu, select format 1, and click OK.

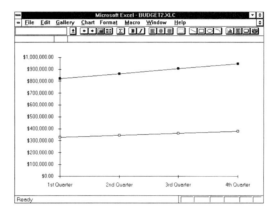

Creating pie charts

3. Choose Pie from the Gallery menu, select format 6, and click OK.

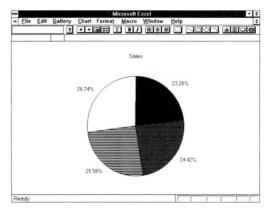

Excel has plotted only one data series in the pie. However, it has not discarded the other data series, as you will see in the next step.

4. Choose 3-D Column from the Gallery menu, select format 4, and click OK.

Creating 3-D charts

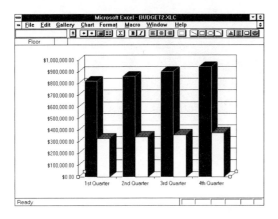

The second data series appears intact, in glorious 3-D.

You might want to spend some time becoming familiar with the other predefined formats so that you have an idea of what's available.

Changing the Preferred Format

When you create a chart, Excel uses the Preferred format, which by default is a plain column chart. If the data you work with most often is better presented in a different format, you can change the Preferred format so that, throughout the current session, Excel uses that chart type instead. Here's how to make area charts the Preferred format:

1. Choose Area from the Gallery menu, select format 1, and click OK. The BUDGET2 chart now looks similar to the line chart you saw earlier, except that the area below each line is filled in.

Creating area charts

2. With the area chart on your screen, choose Set Preferred from the Gallery menu.

To check whether Excel has changed the Preferred format:

1. Choose BUDGET.XLS from the Window menu.

2. Holding down the Ctrl key, select the ranges A9:E9 and A11:E11 in the worksheet, and choose New from the File menu.

3. Select Chart, and click OK. Excel plots the two data series—Total Expenses and Net Income—in the new Preferred format, as shown on the next page.

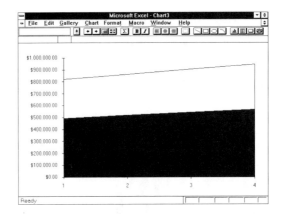

4. Save the new chart with the name BUDGET3.XLC.

Customizing Charts

As we have said, Excel has a predefined format for almost every occasion. However, for those rare times when you need to add an element here or change an element there, the program provides a wealth of formatting options for customizing every conceivable aspect of your charts. We won't go into a lot of detail about formatting here, because we think that Excel's predefined chart types will cover most of your needs. You should know how to add a legend and a title to a chart, however, because they increase the chart's clarity and therefore its persuasiveness.

Adding a Legend

As you saw when you created your first chart at the beginning of this chapter, when you plot a single data series Excel uses the series name as the chart title. When you plot more than one series, however, Excel does not include the series names on the chart, and nothing identifies the respective series. Adding a legend is often the simplest way of eliminating any potential confusion. Here's how to create a legend:

1. With BUDGET3.XLC active on your screen, choose the Add Legend command from the Chart menu. Excel creates a legend using the labels in column A as the series names, as shown here:

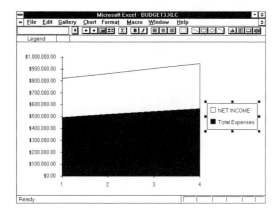

2. While the legend is selected (as indicated by the black handles around its frame), position it aesthetically on the chart by dragging it to the desired location.

Moving legends

3. Make the labels bold by clicking the Bold tool in the Toolbar.

Adding a Title

Because you selected more than one data series when you created BUDGET3.XLC, Excel was unable to determine what the chart's title should be. Here's how you add a title to a multi-series chart:

1. Choose Attach Text from the Chart menu. Excel displays the dialog box shown on the next page.

Adjusting chart data

When your data doesn't need to be exact, you can "fudge" a little to make a column, bar, or line chart or a scatter diagram look better. Hold down Ctrl and click to select the column, bar, or data point you want to change. When a black dot appears, drag it to the desired position. The source data in the worksheet changes accordingly. ♦

Legend labels

If you don't include labels when you select the data to be plotted, Excel assigns the labels Series1, Series2, and so on to the keys in the legend. You then have to change the labels manually. Simply choose Edit Series from the Chart menu. In the Edit Series dialog box, select Series1 in the Series list box, and type the new name in the

Name text box. Then click the Define button. Repeat this process for each label, and then click OK to close the dialog box. ♦

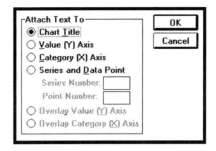

As you can see, you can also use the options in this dialog box to add labels to many elements of the chart.

2. Accept the default selection, Chart Title, by clicking OK. Excel adds the word *Title* at the top of the chart.

3. In the formula bar, replace *Title* with *Expenses by Quarter*, and click the Enter box. Here's the result:

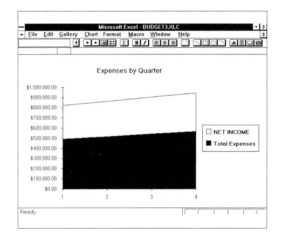

Creating Picture Charts

Graphics in charts

Before we discuss printing charts, we can't resist mentioning a new Excel 3 feature that allows you to use graphics created in programs such as Paintbrush to plot data series in column or bar charts. You start by creating a two-dimensional column or bar chart in Excel. Then you create a simple graphic element in a Windows graphics program and copy it. After activating the Excel chart, you select the series you want the graphic to replace, and choose Paste. Excel then substitutes the graphic for the data-series marker, distorting it to fill the area formerly occupied by the column or bar. You can fill the area with repeating graphics instead, by choosing the Patterns command from the Format menu and selecting one of the Stack options. Here's an example of a picture chart:

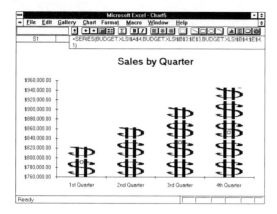

Printing Charts

Printing charts is much like printing worksheets. The main difference concerns the Page Setup dialog box, which allows you to specify whether the chart should be printed the same size as it appears on the screen (Screen Size), enlarged proportionally until it fits within the specified page margins (Fit To Page), or enlarged to fit without regard to width:height ratios (Full Page). You can preview a chart, but because a chart document can never be more than one page, the Next and Previous buttons are not available. Other than that small detail, the basic procedure is the same, and you should have no difficulty obtaining paper copies of your charts.

5

Estimating Project Costs

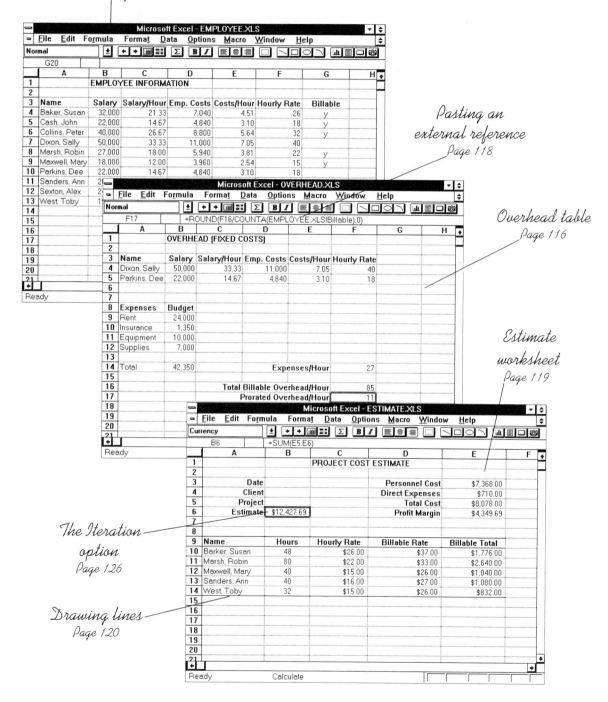

Employee-
information table
Page 115

Pasting an
external reference
Page 118

Overhead table
Page 116

Estimate
worksheet
Page 119

The Iteration
option
Page 126

Drawing lines
Page 120

In this chapter, we tackle a more ambitious set of worksheets. First we create tables of employee information and overhead costs. Then we create a worksheet that estimates project costs by "looking up" hourly rates in one of the tables. Finally, we cover a technique called *iteration*, which enables Excel to resolve circular calculations.

Worksheet ideas

In our example, we create only employee-information and overhead tables because the primary cost involved in the sample project estimate is for people's time. However, you can easily adapt the project cost estimate worksheet to also use a marketing-expenses or materials-information table. For example, if you manage a construction business that specializes in bathroom and kitchen remodeling, you can create a table with up-to-date prices for fixtures, plumbing supplies, cabinets, tile, and so on, in addition to the employee-information and overhead tables. Even if you are a one-person operation and have no employees, you can still adapt the worksheet to make sure that you include overhead and marketing costs in your project estimates.

This chapter differs from previous chapters in that we don't bog down the instructions with information you already know. For example, we might show you a worksheet and ask you to create it, without telling you step-by-step what to enter, how to make an entry bold, and how to adjust column widths. We leave it up to you to create the worksheet using the illustration as a guide. Similarly, we might tell you to create a formula, assuming that you know how to paste a function into a cell (to review the procedure, turn to page 51) and how to click cells to use their references as arguments (see page 38).

Creating the Supporting Tables

The logical way to begin this example is to enter the data needed for the two supporting tables. There's nothing complicated about these tables; we've stripped them down so that you don't have to type any extraneous information. The few calculations involved have been greatly simplified and do not reflect the gyrations accountants would go through to ensure to-the-penny accuracy. So instead of describing step-by-step how to create these tables, we'll simply show them to you and, after discussing the few formulas and cell and range names involved, let you create them on your own.

1. In a blank worksheet, create this table of employee information, and then save it as EMPLOYEE.XLS:

*Employee-
information table*

Microsoft Excel - EMPLOYEE.XLS							
File Edit Formula Format Data Options Macro Window Help							
Normal							
G20							
	A	B	C	D	E	F	G	H
1	EMPLOYEE INFORMATION						
2							
3	Name	Salary	Salary/Hour	Emp. Costs	Costs/Hour	Hourly Rate	Billable
4	Baker, Susan	32,000	21.33	7,040	4.51	26	y
5	Cash, John	22,000	14.67	4,840	3.10	18	y
6	Collins, Peter	40,000	26.67	8,800	5.64	32	y
7	Dixon, Sally	50,000	33.33	11,000	7.05	40	
8	Marsh, Robin	27,000	18.00	5,940	3.81	22	y
9	Maxwell, Mary	18,000	12.00	3,960	2.54	15	y
10	Parkins, Dee	22,000	14.67	4,840	3.10	18	
11	Sanders, Ann	20,000	13.33	4,400	2.82	16	y
12	Sexton, Alex	24,000	16.00	5,280	3.38	19	y
13	West, Toby	19,000	12.67	4,180	2.68	15	y
14							
15							
16							
17							
18							
19							
20							
21							

Ready

Row 4 of this worksheet uses these formulas:

C4   =B4/50/30
      *Annual salary divided by 50 weeks (allowing
      2 weeks for vacation), divided by 30 billable
      hours per week (allowing 2 hours per day of non-
      billable time)*

D4   =B4*22%
      *Employer contributions to social security and
      benefits estimated at 22 percent of annual salary*

E4   =D4/52/30
      *Employer contributions to social security and
      benefits divided by 52 weeks divided by
      30 hours per week*

F4   =ROUND(C4+E4,0)
      *Salary per hour plus benefits per hour, rounded
      to a whole number (0 decimal places)*

*The ROUND
function*

2. After entering these formulas, use Fill Down to copy them to rows 5 through 13.

3. Use Define Name to assign the name Billable to cells G4:G14 and the name Emp_Rate to cells A4:F14. (See

Overhead table ——→

page 39 for information about how to assign range names.) We'll use these names in future formulas.

4. Open a new worksheet, create this overhead table, and save the worksheet as OVERHEAD.XLS:

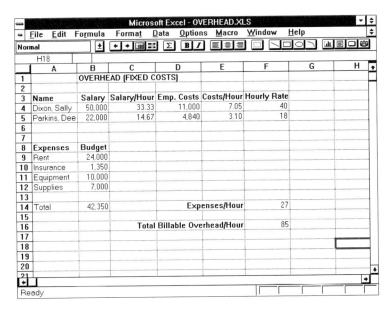

Sally Dixon and Dee Parkins are administrative employees who do not directly generate income for the company, so we need to include their salaries and benefits in this overhead calculation. You can copy their entries from the EMPLOYEE.XLS worksheet or enter them from scratch. Here are the formulas to use in row 4:

Ascending order

You can list employees in any order in the employee-information table, but before Excel can use the table to look up information, you must sort it in ascending order. Excel cannot look up information in randomly ordered tables or in tables in descending order. Select the range and choose the Sort command from the Data menu to sort the table. ♦

Extending range names

It is a good idea to always include a blank cell at the end of the range when assigning range names. If you need to add employees to the EMPLOYEE.XLS worksheet, for example, you can select the blank row below the last entry and choose the Insert command from the Edit menu to extend the range with the name Billable. ♦

Flexible formulas

Keep in mind that using names in formulas makes your worksheets much more flexible than if you use cell references. If the information referenced in a formula moves because of changes you make to a worksheet, Excel adjusts the definition of the name so that it continues to access the correct information. ♦

C4	=B4/50/30
D4	=B4*22%
E4	=D4/52/30
F4	=ROUND(C4+E4,0)

5. If you are entering the formulas from scratch, use Fill Down to copy the entries in row 4 to row 5.

6. Next, enter these formulas in the designated cells:

B14	=SUM(B9:B12)
F14	=ROUND(B14/52/30,0)
F16	=SUM(F4:F14)

We must bill 30 hours each week at the rate in F16 to cover overhead costs. We cannot bill overhead to a client directly, so we must increase the hourly rate of employees with billable hours by a prorated amount to ensure that overhead is included in project estimates. To calculate the prorated overhead amount, we need to divide the total billable rate per hour in cell F16 by the number of employees who generate income. We can glance at the employee-information worksheet and know that this number is eight, but what if the company had many employees? We would want Excel to supply this number for us. Here's how.

Counting Entries

We can tell Excel to count the number of employees that have a Y in the Billable column of EMPLOYEE.XLS by using the COUNTA function. This function has only one argument,

---

Quick argument selection

If you double-click a cell containing a formula, Excel highlights the first cell or range that appears in the formula. In the above example, double-clicking B14 causes Excel to highlight B9:B12 in the formula bar. Double-clicking F14 causes Excel to highlight B14. ◆

Cell notes

To annotate a cell to explain its contents, select the cell, and choose Note from the Formula menu. In the Note section of the Cell Note dialog box, type a sentence or two explaining the cell, and then click OK. Excel displays a small square in the top-right corner of the cell to indicate that a note is attached. Double-click the cell to display the note. ◆

COUNTA vs. COUNT

Don't confuse the COUNTA function with the COUNT function. COUNTA tells you how many cells in the selected range contain entries, whereas COUNT tells you how many cells in the range contain numeric values. ◆

*The COUNTA
function*

which is the range of cells we want Excel to scan for entries. Here's how to use COUNTA in the formula that calculates the overhead allocation:

1. In cell E17 of OVERHEAD.XLS, type *Prorated Overhead/Hour*, click the Enter box, and then click the Bold and Right alignment buttons.

2. We want the prorated amount to be in whole dollars, so we need to nest the prorated calculation in a ROUND function. In cell F17, type the following:

   =ROUND(F16/COUNTA(

*Pasting an
external reference*

To divide the hourly overhead in cell F16 by the number of employees whose hours are billable, choose the EMPLOYEE.XLS worksheet from the Window menu, and then choose the Paste Name command from the Formula menu. Excel displays this dialog box:

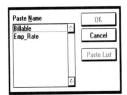

Select Billable, and click OK. Excel follows the open parenthesis in the formula bar with an external reference to the range named Billable in the EMPLOYEE.XLS

Easy opening of linked worksheets

Although Excel will update external references without opening the referenced worksheets, you can easily open all supporting worksheets by choosing the Links command from the File menu. Excel displays a dialog box listing all documents that are referred to by formu-

las in the active worksheet. Simply select the files you want to open, and click the Open button. ♦

More commands

Pressing the Shift key before you pull down menus can change some commands. For example, the Close command on the File menu becomes Close All when you hold down the Shift key, and the Fill Right and Fill Down commands on the Edit menu become Fill Left and Fill Up. ♦

worksheet, thereby linking the two worksheets. Next, type a) to close the COUNTA function. Then type a comma, a zero, and a final) to close the ROUND function.

3. Check that the following function is in the formula bar:

=ROUND(F16/COUNTA(EMPLOYEE.XLS!Billable),0)

and then click the Enter box. Excel calculates the formula and enters the value 11 in cell F17.

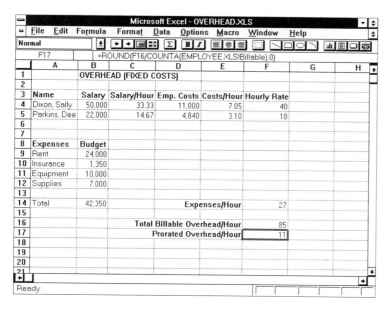

4. Assign the name Over_Rate to cell F17.

Creating the Estimate Worksheet

With the two tables in place, we're ready to create the worksheet for estimating project costs. We'll put the basic structure of the worksheet in place first, and then we'll fill in the formulas necessary for the calculations.

1. Begin by creating the top area of the worksheet, as shown on the next page.

The estimate worksheet

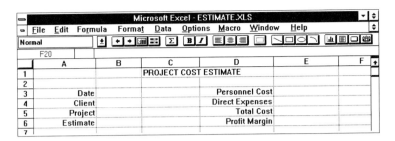

2. Next, enter these headings for the table where we'll calculate the personnel costs of the project:

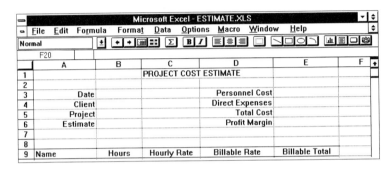

Drawing lines →

3. Draw a line above and below the headings by selecting A9:E9, choosing Border from the Format menu, selecting Top and Bottom, and clicking OK.

4. Now enter the employee names and the number of hours you anticipate each will need to work on this project. Finally, draw a line below the last row of entries by selecting A15:E15, choosing Border from the Format menu, selecting Top, and clicking OK.

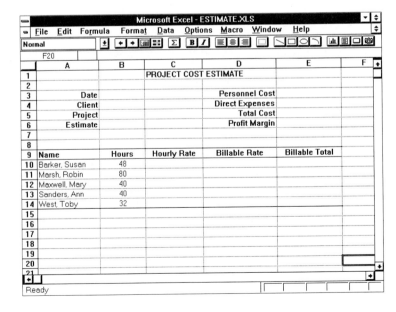

So far, everything has been pretty straightforward and has provided you with nothing more challenging than an opportunity to practice skills you learned in other chapters. Now we need to introduce the Excel function that will enable us to use one of the tables we created earlier to fill in the information needed for this worksheet.

Looking Up Information

Excel has three functions you can use in formulas to look up information in worksheet tables: LOOKUP (a generic function), VLOOKUP (which is for vertically oriented tables), and HLOOKUP (which is for horizontally oriented tables). Here, we'll show you how to use LOOKUP.

Excel needs two pieces of information to carry out the LOOKUP function: the value you want it to look up and the location of the lookup table. You supply these two pieces of information in this way:

The LOOKUP function

=LOOKUP(*value to look for,range to look in*)

If the lookup table has more rows than columns, Excel assumes that it is to search the leftmost column of the table for the value you supply and then enter in the worksheet the value that is in the rightmost column of the table on the same row. For example, to look up the hourly rate for John Cash

Hiding windows	Controlling lookup	Borders around tables
Use the Hide command on the Window menu to hide the active window. For example, you might want to hide windows before choosing Arrange All. If the window is a macro sheet, all macros on the sheet are active even though it is not visible. (See page 141 for more information about macro sheets.) Choose Unhide to make the window reappear. ♦	If the employee-information table had more columns than rows, we would need to use the VLOOKUP function instead of the LOOKUP function in order to force Excel to search the leftmost column for the supplied value instead of the top row. ♦	If you draw borders around tables to set them apart in a worksheet, always create the bottom border by choosing the row below the last row of the table and adding a border to the top of this range. Otherwise, actions such as choosing Fill Down will delete the border. ♦

in the employee-information table, you can enter this function, say in cell A19 of EMPLOYEE.XLS:

=LOOKUP("Cash, John",A4:F13)

Because the employee-information table has more rows than columns, Excel scans the leftmost column—column A—for the text value Cash, John. When it finds the value it's looking for in cell A5, it looks along row 5 to the rightmost column and displays in cell A19 the value 18 from cell F5.

If the employee-information table had more columns than rows, Excel would look for the value you supply in the top row of the table and would enter in the formula cell the value that is in the bottom row of the same column.

Let's see how to put the LOOKUP function to work in the project cost estimate worksheet:

1. Select cell C10 of ESTIMATE.XLS, and choose Paste Function from the Formula menu.

2. Scroll down to the LOOKUP function, select it, check that the Paste Arguments option is selected, and click OK. Click OK in the Select Arguments dialog box. Excel enters the function in the formula bar with the first argument highlighted.

3. Click cell A10, which contains the name of the first employee whose hourly rate we want to look up. The cell reference replaces the first argument in the LOOKUP function in the formula bar.

4. Highlight the LOOKUP function's second argument.

5. Choose EMPLOYEE.XLS from the Window menu, and choose Paste Name from the Formula menu. In the Paste Name dialog box, select Emp_Rate, and click OK. Excel replaces the LOOKUP function's second argument with an external reference to the name assigned to the lookup table in EMPLOYEE.XLS.

6. Click the Enter button. Excel looks up the value in cell A10 (Barker, Susan) in the table called Emp_Rate in EMPLOYEE.XLS and enters the corresponding hourly rate, as shown here:

```
═                        Microsoft Excel - ESTIMATE.XLS              ▼ ↕
═  File  Edit  Formula  Format  Data  Options  Macro  Window  Help        ↕
 Currency        ±  ◆ ◆ ▦ ▒  Σ  B I  ▤▥▦  ☐  ◥◻◌◝  ⊞▤▢◙
    C10            =LOOKUP(A10,EMPLOYEE.XLS!Emp_Rate)
         A          B         C            D              E          F  ↕
 1                      PROJECT COST ESTIMATE
 2
 3            Date                    Personnel Cost
 4           Client                   Direct Expenses
 5          Project                      Total Cost
 6         Estimate                    Profit Margin
 7
 8
 9  Name           Hours  Hourly Rate  Billable Rate  Billable Total
 10 Barker, Susan    48      $26.00
 11 Marsh, Robin     80
 12 Maxwell, Mary    40
 13 Sanders, Ann     40
 14 West, Toby       32
 15
 16
 17
 18
 19
 20
 21                                                               ↓
 ◆                                                             →
 Ready
```

7. Now all you have to do is select cells C10:C14 in ESTIMATE.XLS and choose Fill Down from the Edit menu to enter equivalent formulas that look up the hourly rates for the other people who will be involved in this project.

Completing the Estimate

Well, the hard part is over. A few simple calculations, and you'll be ready to prepare an estimate for your client.

1. In ESTIMATE.XLS, enter these formulas in the indicated cells:

   D10   =C10+OVERHEAD.XLS!Over_Rate
   E10   =B10*D10

2. Use Fill Down to copy the formulas to D11:E14.

Now you can calculate total costs in the summary area at the top of the worksheet:

1. Make these entries in the indicated cells:

   E3   =SUM(G10:G14)
   E4   710
   E5   =G3+G4

   The entry in cell G4 is an estimate of charges that will be incurred for long-distance phone calls, delivery services, and other expenses attributable directly to this project.

As you can see, this worksheet is almost complete:

	A	B	C	D	E	F
			Microsoft Excel - ESTIMATE.XLS			
	File	Edit	Formula	Format	Data	Options	Macro	Window	Help
	Normal								
	F20						
1			PROJECT COST ESTIMATE			
2						
3	Date			Personnel Cost	$7,368.00	
4	Client			Direct Expenses	$710.00	
5	Project			Total Cost	$8,078.00	
6	Estimate			Profit Margin		
7						
8						
9	Name	Hours	Hourly Rate	Billable Rate	Billable Total	
10	Barker, Susan	48	$26.00	$37.00	$1,776.00	
11	Marsh, Robin	80	$22.00	$33.00	$2,640.00	
12	Maxwell, Mary	40	$15.00	$26.00	$1,040.00	
13	Sanders, Ann	40	$16.00	$27.00	$1,080.00	
14	West, Toby	32	$15.00	$26.00	$832.00	
15						
16						
17						
18						
19						
20						
21						
Ready						

Projecting Profit Margin with Iteration

Probably the most difficult part of estimating a project is figuring out the profit margin. We now have a good idea what this project is going to cost. But suppose we need a margin of roughly 35 percent of the estimate total to be sure we make a profit. How do we calculate the actual profit margin when we don't yet know the estimate total, and how do we calculate the estimate total when we don't know the profit margin? We could go in circles forever.

Fortunately, we can have Excel go in circles for us. Using the iteration technique, we can force Excel to calculate the margin formula over and over until it can give us an answer. Follow these steps:

1. Select cell E6, and enter this formula:

    =35%*B6

2. Select cell B6, and enter this formula:

    =SUM(E5:E6)

When you enter the second formula, Excel displays this message box:

After you click OK, the message *Circular:E6* appears in the message bar, telling you that the formula in E6 is the culprit. It multiplies the sum of cells E5 and E6 (the formula in cell B6) by 35 percent. Excel cannot arrive at a result because when it adds E5 and E6, the formula in E6 must be recalculated; and when Excel recalculates the formula, E6 changes, so E5 and E6 must be added again; and so on, forever.

Circular references

Here's how to force Excel to come up with an answer:

1. Choose Calculation from the Options menu. Excel displays this dialog box:

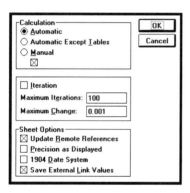

Zero result

When a worksheet contains a circular reference, Excel usually displays 0 as the result of the formula, even if you make adjustments to the values. ◆

Worksheet recalculation

Every time you open a worksheet, Excel recalculates it. When Excel recalculates a worksheet that contains a circular reference, the program always displays the *Cannot resolve circular references* message. ◆

Manual calculation

The Manual Calculation option tells Excel to calculate open worksheets only when you choose the Calculate Now command from the Options menu. You can activate this option for large worksheets, where recalculating each formula can take some time. The Recalculate Before Save option is selected by default when you turn on manual calculation. ◆

The Iteration option

2. Select the Iteration option, and click OK. You return to the worksheet, where Excel quickly recalculates the formulas, finally coming up with these results:

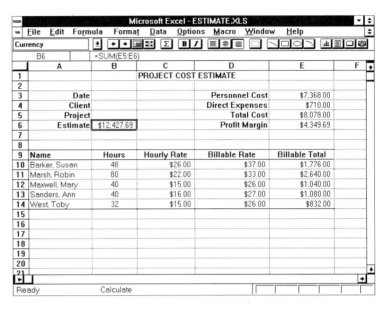

By selecting the Iteration option, you tell Excel to ignore the circular reference and to keep recalculating the formula, going in circles until it comes up with the best possible results. By default, Excel recalculates the formulas 100 times or until the values change by less than .001. The result might not be exact, but inaccuracies of less than a penny are not likely to cause concern.

Date calculation

Excel calculates values for dates as the number of days that have elapsed between January 1, 1900 and the date you specify. If you enter 2-Jan-1900 in a cell, the date has a value of 2, meaning that it is the second day following the base date. If you plan to transfer worksheets containing dates to Excel for the Macintosh, you must choose the Calculation dialog box's 1904 Date System option. Selecting this option recalculates dates on a base date of January 2, 1904. ◆

Precision of values

The Precision As Displayed option tells Excel to use the value displayed in the cell in formulas rather than the underlying value. For example, if a formula refers to a cell that holds the value 15.386, but displays 15.4 because of column width, this option tells Excel to use 15.4 in the formula. ◆

You now have a completed project estimate that takes into account your company's overhead costs as well as the direct costs associated with the project. As we said at the beginning of the chapter, you can adapt this set of worksheets in many ways to help you quickly assemble bids. You can also use the worksheets to compare the cost of doing projects in-house with estimates that you receive from vendors. And once you have set up a lookup table such as the employee-information table, you can link it to worksheets that perform a variety of other personnel-related calculations.

6

Time-Saving Techniques

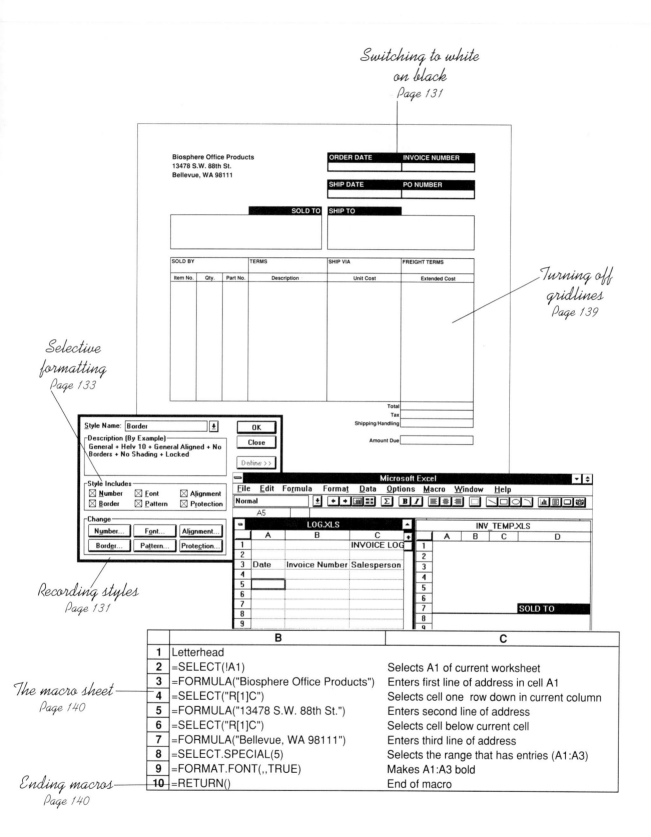

Switching to white
on black
Page 131

Biosphere Office Products
13478 S.W. 88th St.
Bellevue, WA 98111

ORDER DATE	INVOICE NUMBER

SHIP DATE	PO NUMBER

SOLD TO	SHIP TO

SOLD BY	TERMS	SHIP VIA	FREIGHT TERMS

Item No.	Qty.	Part No.	Description	Unit Cost	Extended Cost

	Total
	Tax
Shipping/Handling	
Amount Due	

Turning off
gridlines
Page 139

Selective
formatting
Page 133

Style Name: Border

OK

Close

Define >>

Description (By Example)
General + Helv 10 + General Aligned + No
Borders + No Shading + Locked

Style Includes
☒ Number   ☒ Font   ☒ Alignment
☒ Border   ☒ Pattern   ☒ Protection

Change
Number...   Font...   Alignment...
Border...   Pattern...   Protection...

Recording styles
Page 131

Microsoft Excel

File   Edit   Formula   Format   Data   Options   Macro   Window   Help

Normal

A5

LOG.XLS

	A	B	C
1			INVOICE LOG
2			
3	Date	Invoice Number	Salesperson
4			
5			
6			
7			
8			
9			

INV_TEMP.XLS

	A	B	C	D
1				
2				
3				
4				
5				
6				
7			SOLD TO	
8				
9				

The macro sheet
Page 140

Ending macros
Page 140

	B	C
1	Letterhead	
2	=SELECT(!A1)	Selects A1 of current worksheet
3	=FORMULA("Biosphere Office Products")	Enters first line of address in cell A1
4	=SELECT("R[1]C")	Selects cell one row down in current column
5	=FORMULA("13478 S.W. 88th St.")	Enters second line of address
6	=SELECT("R[1]C")	Selects cell below current cell
7	=FORMULA("Bellevue, WA 98111")	Enters third line of address
8	=SELECT.SPECIAL(5)	Selects the range that has entries (A1:A3)
9	=FORMAT.FONT(,,TRUE)	Makes A1:A3 bold
10	=RETURN()	End of macro

In this final chapter, we discuss two techniques that can greatly increase your efficiency by automating some of the routine tasks associated with setting up worksheets. First, we show you how to create styles to take the tedium out of applying formats. Then we tackle macros. Once you grasp the similarities between styles and macros, even those of you whose palms get sweaty at the thought of having to deal with something as "techie" as a macro programming language will begin thinking of ways to put macros to use.

The example for this chapter is an invoice. In Chapter 3, we said we would show you a way to avoid having to manually input data into databases like invoice logs. The key to streamlining the data-input process is to generate forms such as invoices in Excel and then use a macro to make Excel do the work of transferring the data from the invoices to the invoice log.

The invoice we are going to create in this chapter is shown on the previous page. Take a quick look to get oriented, and then let's get going.

Creating Styles

As you know, to apply a style to the active cell, you simply select it from the Style drop-down list box on the Toolbar. In previous chapters, we applied the Currency and Percentage styles. You can expand the list of available styles by using the Style command on the Format menu to define your own combination of formatting as a style.

Before we create a custom style, let's set up a new template worksheet:

1. Open a new worksheet, and save it as a template with the name INVOICE.XLT. (To save a worksheet in the template format, click the Options button in the Save As dialog box, and select Template from the File Format drop-down list box.)

2. Make the following entries in the indicated cells:

F1	ORDER DATE
G1	INVOICE NUMBER
F4	SHIP DATE
G4	PO NUMBER
D7	SOLD TO
F7	SHIP TO

3. Adjust the column widths as follows:

A, B, C	6.57
D, F, G	20
E	1

Next, we'll apply various formats to the entry in cell F1. We can then define the formats as a style that we can later apply to the other entries.

1. Select cell F1, and choose Font from the Format menu. Next, select the Bold option, and then select the White color swatch from the Color drop-down list box. Click OK. On the worksheet, the entry in cell F1 seems to have disappeared, because it is white in a white cell.

Switching to white on black

2. To make the entry reappear, you need to add shading to the cell. With F1 still selected, choose Patterns from the Format menu, select the Black color swatch from the Foreground drop-down list box, and click OK. The text reappears as white letters in a black cell.

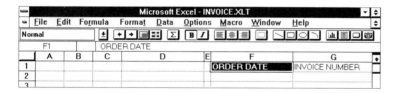

Defining Styles Based on Cell Formatting

Now let's define a style called Reverse based on the formatting in cell F1 and then apply it to other cells.

1. With cell F1 still selected, choose Style from the Format menu. Excel displays this dialog box:

Recording styles

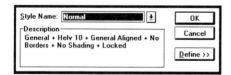

As you can see, in the Description area, Excel displays details of the Normal style's formatting.

2. Type *Reverse*. Excel changes the description to include the formatting you applied to the cell. However, the cell is still formatted with the Normal style.

3. Click OK. The Style list box now displays Reverse as the style applied to cell F1.

Applying custom styles

You apply a custom style the same way that you apply Excel's predefined ones. Let's apply the new style now.

1. Select cell G1, hold down the Ctrl key, and select cells F4, G4, D7, and F7.
2. Pull down the Style list box, and select Reverse.
3. Click any blank cell so that you can see the results.

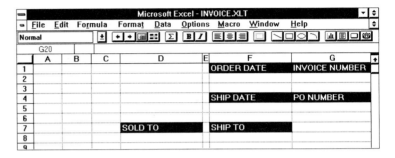

Defining Styles from Scratch

You can create a style from scratch instead of using formatting that you've already applied to a cell. Let's see how this works by creating more styles for INVOICE.XLT.

The Border Style   The first style we'll define from scratch will put a thick border around the selected cell.

1. With a blank cell selected, choose Style from the Format menu. In the Style dialog box, Normal is the entry in the Style Name text box, and the Description box shows the definition of the default Normal style.

Merging styles

A custom style does not take up permanent residence in the Style list box. It appears in the list box only when the worksheet in which you created the style is active. However, you can copy styles between worksheets. Open both the worksheet that contains the style and the worksheet to which you want to copy the style. Then, with the destination worksheet active, choose Style from the Format menu, click the Define button, and then click the Merge button in the expanded Style dialog box. Excel lists the currently open worksheets. Select the source worksheet, and click OK. Excel copies the styles from the source worksheet to the destination worksheet. ◆

Quick style definition

A quick way to define a style is to format the cell, and then type the name for the new style directly in the Style list box on the Toolbar. All you have to do is highlight the current style name, and type in the new name. ◆

2. Type *Border* in the Style Name text box, and click the
    Define button. Excel expands the Style dialog box to
    include several options:

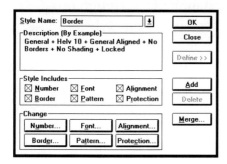

3. You want this style to apply a border to a selected cell
    without disturbing any existing formatting, so in the
    Style Includes area, be sure that all the options except
    Border are deselected.

    Selective formatting

4. In the Change area, Border is now the only available
    button. Click it to display this Border dialog box:

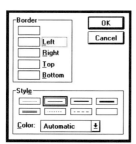

Direct dialog-box access

The buttons in the Change
area of the expanded Style
dialog box display the dialog
boxes you see if you choose
the corresponding command
from the Format menu. For
example, when defining a
style, you can access the
Alignment dialog box by
choosing Alignment from
the Format menu or by clicking the Alignment button in
the Style dialog box. ♦

A Date style

Another likely candidate for
a style is the date format you
use most frequently. Simply
select a cell to which you
have applied the date format,
choose Styles, give the style
a name, such as Date, and
click OK. ♦

Quick style changes

A quick way to redefine a
style is to select a cell that is
formatted with the style you
want to change and then
make the changes to the format of that cell. Next, select
the style from the Style list
box. Excel asks whether you
want to redefine the style
based on the formatting of
the selected cell. Click Yes to
redefine the style. ♦

5. In the Border dialog box, select the thickest border option, and then select Left, Right, Top, and Bottom. Click OK. The Style dialog box now displays the format you selected in the Description box.

6. Click OK again. The style's name has been added to the Style list box on the Toolbar.

Removing formats

7. Remove the border from the cell used to create this style by choosing Clear from the Edit menu. Select the Formats option to clear the border format, and then click OK.

Now we can apply the Border style to the headings in INVOICE.XLT, including the cells below them in the selections to define areas for data entry. Try this:

1. Select F1:G2, hold down Ctrl, and select F4:G5.

2. Select Border from the Style drop-down list box. Click a blank cell to see the result:

```
┌─────────────────────────────────────────────────────────────┐
│ ═      Microsoft Excel - INVOICE.XLT                    ▼ ▲  │
│ ▫ File  Edit  Formula  Format  Data  Options  Macro  Window  Help │
│ Normal        ± ◄ ► ▦ ⊞ Σ B I ≡ ≣ ≣ □ ◺ ▢ ○ ◿ ▥ ▤ ▢ ▨ │
│    G19                                                        │
│       B       C        D       E       F            G     H  │
│  1                                    ORDER DATE   INVOICE NUMBER │
│  2                                                            │
│  3                                                            │
│  4                                    SHIP DATE    PO NUMBER  │
│  5                                                            │
│  6                                                            │
└─────────────────────────────────────────────────────────────┘
```

So far, creating styles has been an interesting exercise, but all we've done is taken a roundabout route to formatting when the direct route would have been more efficient. So what's the big deal about styles? Let's find out:

Changing styles

1. Select cell F2, and choose Style from the Format menu.

2. In the Style dialog box, click the Define button, and then click the Border button in the Change area.

3. Change the line to the second thickest width, and then reselect Left, Right, Top, and Bottom.

4. Click OK twice to close the dialog boxes.

Back on the worksheet, Excel has changed all the cells with the Border style to reflect the new style definition. One change in one place produces instant results throughout the entire worksheet.

The Small Style   Before we create another style, we need to finish the headings for the invoice, like this:

1. Make the following entries in the indicated cells, using the capitalization shown. Click the Bold button on the Toolbar after you make each entry.

A13	SOLD BY
D13	TERMS
F13	SHIP VIA
G13	FREIGHT TERMS
A15	Item No.
B15	Qty.
C15	Part No.
D15	Description
F15	Unit Cost
G15	Extended Cost
F30	Total
F31	Tax
F32	Shipping/Handling
F34	Amount Due

2. Select row 15, and click the Center Alignment button on the Toolbar.

3. Select F30:F34, and click the Right Alignment button.

Now for the next custom style. Because the columns of the invoice are not very wide, let's create a style that will make the invoice entries small:

1. With a blank cell selected, choose Style from the Format menu. Type *Small* in the Style Name text box, and click the Define button.

2. In the expanded Style dialog box, be sure that all the options except Font are deselected in the Style Includes area, and then click Font in the Change area to display the Font dialog box.

3. Select 8 in the Size area, then select the Bold option, and click OK. When the Style dialog box reappears, click OK again.

Now let's apply the Small style to the data entry areas of INVOICE.XLT:

1. Select the following ranges, holding down Ctrl to add each successive range to the selection:

F2:G2	A8:D11
F5:G5	F8:G11
A13:G34	

2. Select Small from the Style list box. The size of the headings changes, but you won't notice dramatic results until you enter information in the invoice.

Before we move on, let's take care of a few more formatting details:

1. Because you will be entering dates in two of the boxes at the top of the screen, let's format them now. While holding down the Ctrl key, select cells F2 and F5. Then choose Number from the Format menu, select the m/d/yy format, and click OK. (If you now create a Date style, you can apply the date format to other cells with a simple click of the mouse.)

2. Format the cells in the Unit Cost and Extended Cost columns as dollars and cents by selecting them and then selecting Currency from the Style list box.

Now that we've gotten our feet wet with styles, let's take a look at macros, which are conceptually similar to styles but much more powerful.

Creating Macros

An Excel macro is a set of instructions. When you run a macro, Excel moves sequentially through the instructions, doing whatever it is told to do. The instructions are written on a macro sheet that resembles a worksheet, in a form

---

Style changes

Although you can instantly change the formatting of many cells in a worksheet by redefining the style, you can change only the most recently applied style. For example, suppose you apply the Reverse style to a cell and then apply the Border style. The Reverse style is still visible in the cell, but the Border style appears in the Style list box on the Toolbar when you click the cell. You can change the Border style, and your changes will be reflected in the cell, but if you make changes to the Reverse style, those changes will not affect the cell. If you want changes you make to the Reverse style to appear in the cell, you must format the cell manually. ♦

Wide columns

The cells in macro sheets are wider than those in worksheets, because the Formulas option is selected in the Display dialog box. By default, Excel displays formulas, not their results, in macro sheets. ♦

similar to the functions you enter in the formula bar. For example, this macro function

=SELECT(!C5)

tells Excel to select cell C5 on the active worksheet. (If you don't include the !, Excel selects C5 on the macro sheet.)

To make it easy for new users to start creating macros right away, Excel has a macro recorder that enables you to record a series of keystrokes and commands as a macro. Excel takes care of translating the keystrokes and commands into the macro language and writing them on the macro sheet. You assign the macro a name and then "play it back" simply by opening the macro sheet and choosing the Run command from the Macro menu and selecting the name in the Run dialog box. You can also designate a shortcut key combination that you can press to run the macro. You can even link the macro to a "button" that you have created on the worksheet using one of Excel's new graphics tools; simply clicking the button runs the macro.

Macro recorder

Our discussion of macros will be necessarily brief and is not intended to make you an instant Excel macro expert. The idea is to get you thinking about whether tasks you perform routinely could be more efficiently carried out with macros, and to give you enough information to explore the topic further on your own. We start by showing you how to record a macro. Next, we take a look at macro sheets and the process by which you create macros from scratch. Then we assign a macro to a button. Finally, we examine a macro that transfers information from a filled-out invoice to an invoice log.

Recording Macros

To look like the invoice at the beginning of the chapter, the invoice now on your screen needs borders around several ranges. Why can't we use the Border style we created earlier in the chapter to draw a border around those cells? To see why not, try it:

1. Select A8:D11, and select Border from the Style list box. Instead of outlining the whole range, Excel puts a border around each individual cell.

2. Choose Undo Style from the Edit menu.

To outline the entire range, we must select the range, choose Border from the Format menu, select Outline in the

Border dialog box, and click OK. This set of steps is an ideal candidate for a recorded macro, so let's get to work.

The Outline macro

1. Select A8:D11, the first range you want to outline.
2. Turn on the macro recorder by choosing Record from the Macro menu. Excel displays this dialog box:

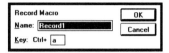

3. Type *Outline* as the name of the macro, and press Tab to move to the Key text box.
4. To be able to run the macro simply by pressing Ctrl-o, type *o* in the Key text box. Then click OK. Excel opens a macro sheet behind the current worksheet and begins recording. From now until you turn off the recorder, Excel will record every action you take.
5. Choose Border from the Format menu, select the second thickest line, select Outline, and click OK.
6. Choose Stop Recorder from the Macro menu to stop the recorder.

In the course of creating the macro, we have outlined the selected range. Now let's use the Outline macro to format the next range:

1. Select F8:G11.

The Run command

2. Choose Run from the Macro menu. Excel displays this dialog box:

Smart recorder	**Correct syntax**	**Halting macros**
If you cancel an action, or click Cancel in a dialog box while Excel is recording a macro, the action is not recorded. ♦	If you don't enter a function with perfect syntax, Excel displays an error message and highlights the offending section of the function in the formula bar. Refer to the *Microsoft Excel Function Reference* for the correct macro function syntax. ♦	You can halt a macro's progress at any point by simply clicking the Esc button. Excel displays a dialog box telling you at what cell it stopped the macro. You can then proceed by clicking the Halt, Step, Continue, or Goto buttons. ♦

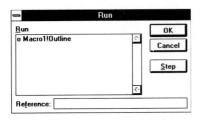

The *o* that precedes the macro name indicates the key
you press with the Ctrl key to activate the macro.

3. Select Macro1!Outline, and click OK. Excel places a
   border around the range.

Now let's use the shortcut key combination to outline
some more ranges:

1. Select A13:C14, and press Ctrl-o.

2. Select the following ranges, pressing Ctrl-o after each
   selection:

D13:E14	F13:F14
G13:G14	A16:A29
B16:B29	C16:C29
D16:E29	F16:F29
G16:G29	

The shortcut key combination

3. Finish off the borders by selecting A15, C15, F15, G15,
   G30:G32, and G34 and then applying the Border style
   from the Style list box.

4. To make the borders stand out, turn off the gridlines
   by choosing Display from the Options menu, deselect-
   ing Gridlines, and clicking OK. Here's the result:

Turning off gridlines

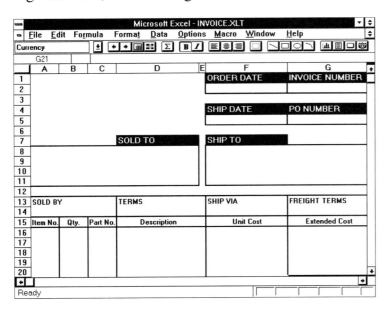

Now would be a good time to save the template again, to preserve the work you have done so far.

Defining Macros from Scratch

You've probably noticed the blank hole in the top-left corner of the invoice. Let's create a simple macro that will insert a company name and address in this area. In the process, we'll take a look at a macro sheet and learn something about the Excel macro language. Follow these steps:

The macro sheet →

1. Choose Macro1 from the Window menu. Excel displays this macro sheet on your screen. (You can widen column A to see the whole macro.)

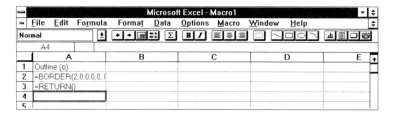

Excel created the Macro1 macro sheet and wrote the macro instructions in column A when you recorded the Outline macro. In cell A1, the name of the macro is followed by the shortcut key you assigned. In cell A2 is the BORDER macro function that creates the range outline. This function has six numeric arguments, each representing one of the options selected in the Border dialog box. So the function

   =BORDER(2,0,0,0,0,,0)

selects a thin outline for the border and leaves all the other options deselected.

Ending macros →

The last function in the macro, =RETURN(), ends the macro. Macros that don't end with RETURN()—or alternatively HALT()— produce error messages.

A thorough examination of Excel's macro functions is beyond the scope of this book. Suffice it to say that an Excel macro function probably exists for every common worksheet task—and for many uncommon ones, too! You can consult the *Microsoft Excel Function Reference* for a complete listing of all the macro functions and their arguments. In the meantime, let's combine a few simple functions to create another macro. Follow these steps:

1. Save Macro1 with the Save As command, assigning it the name GENERAL (for *general-purpose.*) Excel appends the extension XLM.

2. In cell B1 of the macro sheet, type *Letterhead*, the name of this macro.

3. To enter the company name and address, type the following macro functions in the indicated cells, exactly as you see them here. (You can substitute your own company's name and address if you want.) You don't have to type the comments in column C, which explain the action of each function.

	B	C
1	Letterhead	
2	=SELECT(!A1)	Selects A1 of current worksheet
3	=FORMULA("Biosphere Office Products")	Enters first line of address in cell A1
4	=SELECT("R[1]C")	Selects cell one row down in current column
5	=FORMULA("13478 S.W. 88th St.")	Enters second line of address
6	=SELECT("R[1]C")	Selects cell below current cell
7	=FORMULA("Bellevue, WA 98111")	Enters third line of address
8	=SELECT.SPECIAL(5)	Selects the range that has entries (A1:A3)
9	=FORMAT.FONT(,,TRUE)	Makes A1:A3 bold
10	=RETURN()	End of macro

4. Select cell B2, and choose Define Name from the Formula menu to display the following dialog box.

Macro libraries

Having saved a macro sheet, you can use it with many worksheets. For example, you could build a library of general-purpose macros in the GENERAL.XLM macro sheet. If you open that sheet whenever you create a new worksheet, all the general-purpose macros will be available for use. ♦

R1C1 notation

The R1C1 cell referencing scheme references cells by their row and column position in relation to the active cell. The easiest way to understand this notation is with a few examples. If the active cell is B2, RC is the cell in the same row and the same column as the active cell—in other words, it is cell B2, the active cell itself. R[-1]C is the cell in the row above and in the same column as the active cell—in other words, it is cell B1. R[-1]C[-1] is the cell in the row above and one column to the left—in other words, it is cell A1. Similarly, R[1]C[1] is the cell in the row below and one column to the right—cell C3. ♦

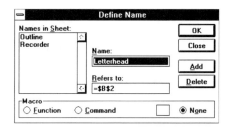

5. Excel suggests the name Letterhead, which is just what we want. Click the Command button, and then type the letter *l* in the Ctrl+ text box. Finally, click OK.

Now let's test the new macro:

1. Choose INVOICE.XLT from the Window menu, and select cell A1.

2. Press Ctrl-l to run the macro. Here's the result:

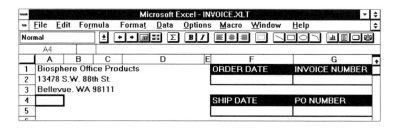

Congratulations. You've just written your first macro.

Importing graphics

To create a really fancy letterhead, you can import a graphic into Excel from any application that supports the METAFILE file format. (See Excel's documentation for more information.) For example, you can create a logo in Paintbrush and paste it into a worksheet, like this: **1.** Switch to Program Manager, and start Paintbrush. Create a small, simple graphic to use as a logo. Use the text tool to add the name and address. Then select the graphic, and copy it. Close Paintbrush, and return to Excel. **2.** Paste the graphic into the active worksheet. The graphic appears, surrounded by a set of handles that you can use to resize the graphic. **3.** Click anywhere within the graphic, and drag it to the desired position on the worksheet.

By default, graphics in Excel move with the cells that are under them, if you insert or delete other cells. Although the cells are hidden by the graphic, they can still contain text or numbers, and can be used in calculations. Worksheet graphics can also function as macro buttons (see page 143 for more information). ♦

Assigning Macros to Buttons

As we mentioned earlier, you can assign a macro to a button on the worksheet and then run the macro simply by clicking the button. You create the button using the Button tool, one of the graphics tools on the Toolbar:

Creating buttons

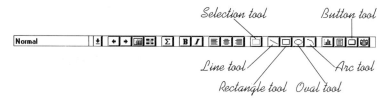

Buttons are useful because they provide instant access to their macros and because they serve as a graphic reminder of the macro's availability.

To see how buttons work, try this:

1. Clear the address from cells A1:A3 of INVOICE.XLT, and click the Button tool.

2. Drag a marquee that covers cells A6:C7. Excel creates a button and displays this dialog box:

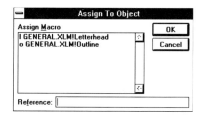

The graphics tools

With Excel's graphics tools, you can create simple graphics, such as a logo for the invoice. The best way to learn how to use the Line, Rectangle, Oval, and Arc tools is to experiment. To create a graphic object, click one of the tools, and drag it over the worksheet. Holding down the Shift key while creating objects constrains lines to 45-degree angles and creates perfect squares, circles, and arcs. Use the handles that surround a selected object to resize it. Choose the Patterns command from the Format menu to adjust the object's line thickness, fill color, and pattern, and to add arrowheads to lines.

Select several objects and use the Group command on the Format menu so that you can manipulate the objects as a group. Use the Send To Back and Bring To Front commands to adjust the order of objects stacked on top of one another

Use the Selection tool on the Toolbar to select graphic objects, and the Text tool to annotate a worksheet with text in a box. ◆

3. The Assign Macro list box lists the macros available in open macro sheets. Select Letterhead, and click OK.
4. With the button selected, highlight the Button 1 label, and type *Address*. (If necessary, use the Selection tool on the Toolbar to select the button.)
5. Click elsewhere on the worksheet to deselect the button, and then click the button to run the Letterhead macro. Here's the result:

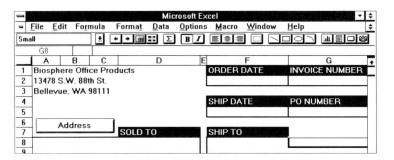

Logging Invoice Data with a Macro

Macro ideas

You now know enough about macros to follow along as we create one that will take the information you enter into a copy of INVOICE.XLT and record it in an invoice log. This macro can be adapted for many uses. For example, you could use the techniques you learned while creating the invoice to develop a contacts template. You could then adapt the macro to pull information about each new client you work with into

---

Macro availability

The macro must be on an open macro sheet. If the macro sheet is not open when you click the button, Excel displays an error message. ♦

Macro button changes

If you need to reassign another macro to the button or you want to change the button name or size, use the Selection tool to select it, or hold down the Ctrl key and click the button. ♦

Graphic macro buttons

As we've said, you can assign macros to any graphic object you create, even a line or a text box. Just select the object or group of objects, and choose Assign To Object from the Macro menu. Excel displays the Assign To Object dialog box. Simply select a macro, and click OK. The next time you click the object, the macro runs. ♦

a name and address database. Or you might want to create an expense-report template and adapt the macro to record expenses in a reimbursement summary.

Before we can work on the macro, we need to create the invoice-log worksheet, so let's get to work.

Setting Up the Invoice Log

For demonstration purposes, we'll keep this log very simple. Follow these steps:

1. Open a new worksheet, and make the following entries in the indicated cells:

C1	INVOICE LOG
A3	Date
B3	Invoice Number
C3	Salesperson
D3	Amount of Sale

2. Select A1:D4, and click the Bold button.

3. Adjust the column widths so that you can see all the entries.

4. We want Excel to append new invoices to the end of the invoice log, so select cell A4, choose Define Name from the Formula menu, type *end*, and click OK.

   Designating the end of a database

5. Save the worksheet with the name LOG.XLS, leaving it open on your screen.

That's it for the log. Now let's move on to create the macro.

Creating the Log Macro

The Log macro we are going to create is a relatively straightforward combination of Copy and Paste commands. Take a little time as you enter the functions to figure out what each one does.

1. Choose New from the File menu, select Macro Sheet, and click OK. Save the new macro sheet as LOG.XLM.

2. Enter the functions on the next page exactly as you see them. (You can copy and paste cells A5:A9 three times and then edit the copies, rather than typing all the entries from scratch.) Again, you don't have to type the comments in column B.

	A	B
1	Log	
2	=FORMULA.GOTO("LOG.XLS!end")	Activate cell named "end" in invoice log
3	=SELECT("R")	Select row containing active cell
4	=INSERT(2)	Insert a new row above selected row
5	=FORMULA.GOTO("INV_TEMP.XLS!R2C6")	Select order date in invoice
6	=COPY()	Copy it
7	=FORMULA.GOTO("LOG.XLS!end")	Activate cell named "end" in invoice log
8	=SELECT("R[-1]C1")	Select column 1 of row above "end"
9	=PASTE.SPECIAL(3,1,FALSE,FALSE)	Paste order date without formatting
10	=FORMULA.GOTO("INV_TEMP.XLS!R2C7")	Select invoice number
11	=COPY()	Copy it
12	=ACTIVATE("LOG.XLS")	Activate invoice log
13	=SELECT("RC2")	Select column 2 of current row
14	=PASTE.SPECIAL(3,1,FALSE,FALSE)	Paste invoice number without formatting
15	=FORMULA.GOTO("INV_TEMP.XLS!R14C1")	Select salesperson's name
16	=COPY()	Copy it
17	=ACTIVATE("LOG.XLS")	Activate invoice log
18	=SELECT("RC3")	Select column 3 of current row
19	=PASTE.SPECIAL(3,1,FALSE,FALSE)	Paste salesperson's name without formatting
20	=FORMULA.GOTO("INV_TEMP.XLS!R34C7")	Select amount of sale
21	=COPY()	Copy it
22	=ACTIVATE("LOG.XLS")	Activate invoice log
23	=SELECT("RC4")	Select column 4 of current row
24	=PASTE.SPECIAL(3,1,FALSE,FALSE)	Paste amount of sale without formatting
25	=RETURN()	End of macro

3. Select cell A2, and choose the Define Name command from the Formula menu. Accept the default name, Log, click the Command button, and then click OK.

4. Save the macro sheet again.

Running the Macro

Now for the acid test. We'll open an invoice, make a few entries, and then run the macro. Here goes:

1. Open a copy of INVOICE.XLT. The Log macro expects the invoice from which it is to transfer data to be called INV_TEMP.XLS, so save the invoice with that temporary name.

2. Enter a date in cell F2, a number in cell G2, a name in cell A14, and a dollar amount in cell G34.

3. Choose LOG.XLS from the Window menu.

4. To see the macro working, resize both LOG.XLS and INV_TEMP.XLS so that they each occupy half of the screen, like this:

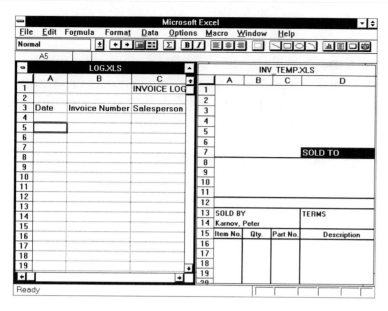

5. Choose Run from the Macro menu, select Log, and click OK. If you have entered the macro correctly, Excel transfers the information you entered to the log as shown here:

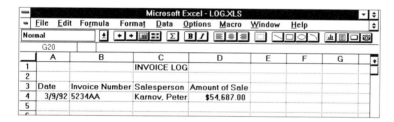

6. Activate the invoice and save it with a new permanent name—the invoice number would be a good choice, as long as it has no more than eight characters.

You might want to create another copy of INVOICE.XLT, name it INV_TEMP.XLS, make a few entries, and run the macro, to see how Excel appends the information from successive invoices to the invoice log.

If the Macro Doesn't Work

If Excel encounters an error in the macro, it stops and displays a message announcing the location of the error. You can then click the Goto button to go directly to the cell on the macro sheet that caused the error. The most likely cause of errors is typos. But if you can't see anything wrong with

Macro error message

the offending function, Excel offers another way to sleuth out the cause of the problem.

Stepping through a macro

In the Run dialog box is a Step option that allows you to step through the macro a function at a time. Selecting a macro from the list and then clicking the Step button displays a small window, like this one:

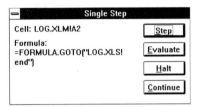

Excel displays the first macro function in the area to the left so that you can examine it. If you click the Step button, Excel executes the displayed function and displays the next function. You thus have the opportunity to see the macro in slow motion and have a better chance of spotting errors.

Well, that quick overview of macros winds up the book. You are now equipped with the tools you need to create some pretty sophisticated worksheets and should be familiar enough with Excel to explore on your own.

Index

Acknowledgments

Our thanks to Jon Ulrigg.

About Online Press

Founded in 1986, Online Press is a group of publishing professionals working to make the presentation and access of information manageable, efficient, accurate, and economical. In 1991 we began publishing our popular *Quick Course* computer-book series, offering streamlined instruction for today's busy professional. At Online Press, it is our goal to help computer users quickly learn what they need to know about today's most popular software programs to get their work done efficiently.

Cover design and photography by Tom Draper Design
Interior text design by Salley Oberlin, Joyce Cox, and Kjell Swedin
Graphics by Patrick Kervran
Proofreading by Polly Fox Urban
Layout by Joyce Cox and Bill Teel
Printed by Viking Press Inc.
Otabind® cover by Muscle Bound Bindery

Text composition by Online Press in Times Roman, with display type in Helvetica Narrow Bold, using Ventura Publisher and the Linotronic 300 laser imagesetter.

Other *Quick Course* Books

Don't miss the other titles in our *Quick Course* series! Quality books at the unbeatable price of $12.95.

Available now...

A Quick Course in Windows
A Quick Course in DOS 5
A Quick Course in WordPerfect 5.1

Coming soon...

A Quick Course in Word for Windows   (November 1991)
A Quick Course in Lotus 1-2-3 for Windows   (Early 1992)
A Quick Course in WordPerfect for Windows   (Early 1992)

Plus more to come...

For our latest catalog, call (206) 641-3434 or write to us at:
Online Press Inc., 14320 NE 21st Street, Suite 18, Bellevue, WA 98007

43a

43c

45

78a

84

Whangarei   23

34

59a

Auckland   54

41

20a

43b

38

Tauranga

60   Hamilton

83   82

101   98

78b   88   20b

100

Rotorua

85

106
107   108
109

110b

110a   27b

27a

L. Taupo   87

15a

104

69
New Plymouth
4

80b

102
111
112

Napier

Hastings   36
66a

68   81

Wanganui

80a

66b
Palmerston North

46

58a

Wellington

56

The Beauty of New Zealand

The Beauty of New Zealand

Robin Smith
Warren Jacobs

with text by Errol Brathwaite

Golden Press
AUCKLAND CHRISTCHURCH SYDNEY

Lake Quill and the Sutherland Falls

Rugged mountains, graceful lakes and snow-fed rivers

To say that New Zealand contains mountains, lakes and rivers would be a gross understatement. Mountains, lakes and rivers in this country are not mere features, but the very shape and essence of the land—forces which play their part in shaping, not only the rest of the non-mountainous and non-riparian New Zealand landscape, but the very character of the country and its peoples. It must be unique, this mere 270 000 square kilometres, in possessing both a variety of scenery which represents practically every type of landscape to be found anywhere in the world, and a population of under 3 000 000 which exhibits a number of regional characteristics.

The old Maori legend has it that the demigod, Maui, went out in a canoe with his brothers, fishing. Maui caught a monstrous fish, hauling it to the surface, whereupon his brothers, catchless and ravenously hungry, leaped on to it and began to eat it there and then. It lies there still, beside the canoe, all slashed and gnawed, with its great backbone exposed.

This 'backbone' begins with the Coromandel Range, high hills rather than mountains, by New Zealand standards, with no peaks of more than 1 000 metres in height. It continues down the Kaimai Range, appears as odd chains of 'vertibrae' on the central volcanic plateau, knots into a tangle of peaks where the Kaimanawas dovetail into the Ruahine Range, and continues, with occasional peaks of almost 2 000 metres, to the Manawatu Gorge, where they are chopped through by the river, on whose right bank the Ruahines terminate in sheer faces and steep slopes, and on whose left bank the Tararua Range rises abruptly and continues in an unbroken chain of 1 000 to 1 700 metre peaks to the head of the 'fish'.

The 'canoe', of course, is the South Island, and has its own mighty mountain chain, higher and grander than the mountains of the North Island, especially along that sector of the massif known as the Southern Alps. Highest of these alpine peaks is Mount Cook named by the Maoris *Aorangi*, the Cloud Piercer, thrusting up to 3,762 metres; and there are more than a hundred and thirty peaks that rise over 2 400 metres.

The South Island mountains have grown slowly, so that rivers have here and there cut into them as they grew. Clearly the volcanic mountains had a very different origin. Where they stand, the entire landscape tends to be dotted with other, similar but smaller swellings, or rent with ancient fissures, and oddly terraced. Rivers have a way of sliding peacefully along a forest floor, to leap suddenly into space and fall into a basin of tortured rock thirty metres below. Lakes on the volcanic plateau tend to be gigantic subsidences, like Taupo, a sheet of extremely deep water 616 square kilometres in area.

The volcanic cones themselves are sometimes beautifully symmetrical. Egmont, for instance, the 2 520-metre dormant volcano on the West Cape of the North Island, is sometimes referred to as New Zealand's Fuji, although its symmetry is somewhat marred by the humped shoulder of Fantham's Peak, which juts out on its southern side. Ngauruhoe, in the centre of the island, is

Lake Mangamahoe and Mount Egmont

Mount Egmont is usually referred to as an extinct volcano. It is actually a dormant volcano, according to vulcanologists.

Balfour Glacier, Mount Cook

One of many glaciers on the slopes of
New Zealand's highest mountain, the
Balfour is fed by the eternal snowfields on
the precipitous flanks of the great pinnacle.
A gleaming river of ice, it is typical of the
scenic splendour of this region.

Mount Cook from Hooker Valley

Mount Cook has been climbed frequently,
though even the easiest routes to the
summit are only for experienced climbers.
This approach leads up the Hooker Valley
to the Hooker Glacier.

Mount Cook, above and opposite

Highest peak in the Southern Alpine chain,
Mount Cook soars 3 762 metres, its massive,
sheer faces perpetually snow-covered and
continuously shedding snow in great,
crashing avalanches. Weather from the
west piles up behind its mighty shoulders, in
the form of a boiling, porridge-like mass of
cloud which seethes and rises under the
pressure of powerful winds, to slop over
the ridges and spill down into the Tasman
Valley. From the darkness at the head of

Lake Pukaki, where the Tasman Valley
opens out into the Mackenzie Basin, the top
of Mount Cook appears to catch fire as the
first rays of the morning sun strike it; and
from that moment on, it presents a
breathtaking display of light, shade, colour
and changing mood throughout the day.

7

another near-perfect cone, though it is entangled in a rent and heaped clutter of peaks and ridges. Its two neighbours, Ruapehu and Tongariro, are not particularly symmetrical at all; or, rather, Ruapehu is, especially from a distance, a shapely cone, but proves to be so rifted with gullies and spurred with minor ridges, as to have the appearance, from some angles, of the skeleton of a cone. Tongariro is a torn, shattered peak, all steaming ponds, boiling streams and fumaroles.

There are other volcanic peaks dotted here and there throughout the country. Pirongia Mountain, in the Waikato, still manages to appear awesomely shattered, despite its softening drapery of rain forest; and the city of Auckland is set on a series of more-or-less perfect minor cones across the Tamaki Peninsula, with the perfectly symmetrical Rangitoto Island guarding the approach to the harbour from the Hauraki Gulf.

In the South Island, Banks Peninsula is a ripped and blasted collection of volcanic cones, the two largest of which blew out with titanic force in recent times, geologically speaking, letting in the sea to form Lyttelton and Akaroa Harbours. From Christchurch, the chain of hills which separate the city from its port are, like Pirongia Mountain, jaggedly shattered, without the softening effect of trees to hide the distorted lava plugs along the crest. From the air, the ancient lava flows can still be seen as they froze, creeping out across the plain and into Lake Ellesmere.

The South Island's alpine chain, structurally similar to the central ranges of the North Island, but on a grander scale, stretches in a more-or-less unbroken wall, from the

Arrow Basin and Remarkables

The Arrow River, rising in the Harris Mountains, snakes through a narrow valley, carved by some ancient glacier, to join the Kawarau not far from Lake Wakatipu. The turbulent stream is fed by little rain- and snow-fed rills, forming a natural irrigation system, greening the Arrow Basin and making it an hospitable area, easy to live in by comparison with the surrounding, desert-like country. The Arrow River was the scene of a massive gold-rush in the 1860s.

drowned valleys which form the Marlborough Sounds, to the sunken glacial valleys which form the Fiords of South Westland. There are branching chains, notably the Kaikouras, the Humboldt Mountains, the Darran Range, the Dart Barrier Range and the Remarkables. The Alps are monstrous serrations, holding long, serpentine lakes entrapped in their folds, and giving birth, in secret valleys, to fierce, snow-fed rivers. The central chain of peaks rears up from a maze of high ridges whose feet are lost in primeval, olive-drab beech forest, which, in some areas and at lower altitudes, gives way to tracts of *totara* and *rimu*, splashed, here and there in due season, with the scarlet of *rata* blossom and the gold of *kowhai*, with, in places, great clouds of yellow where exotic larch turns colour in the early autumn frosts.

The whole area is one of breathtaking beauty, Nature presenting vista after vista of stupendous, snow-mantled heights framed in exquisite sylvan beauty.

But the mountains are crumbling. The lower peaks, which lose their snow in summer, stand revealed as gargantuan gravel heaps— with rocky skeletons, to be sure, but with their mighty flanks eroding at a rate which keeps the long Canterbury rivers gravel-choked and quite unlike rivers anywhere else in the land.

Canterbury rivers can flood with savage power. They can be deep and treacherous; but over much of their length they are tangled skeins of fierce creeks running over gravel beds, sometimes disappearing beneath the gravel for considerable distances.

It is generally said that rivers on this eastern side of the Alps are slow, gravel-choked and meandering, whereas the West Coast rivers are short, swift and deep. But this is a generalization. There are West Coast rivers which wander pleasantly across pastureland and through forests which are almost sub-tropically luxuriant; and there are eastern rivers which flow deep, wide and implacable.

The Mawheraiti River, for example, chatters placidly across Westland pastures and weaves its way through heaped dredge tailings. The Clutha, on the other hand, flows out of an alpine lake, swift, deep and pugnacious, brawling through a dun-coloured countryside where the hills have had their tops planed smooth by Ice Age glaciers and where the rock ribs of the mountains show through the patchy grass; through rock-bound gorges it punches its way, out to lush lowland pastureland where the willows trail long, green fingers in its green water, and only the occasional whirlpools and eddies show how deep and swift the green water is. It divides to flow around a wide, low-lying island before joining up again and surging into the Pacific Ocean. Navigable, though seldom navigated now, it is New Zealand's greatest river in terms of volume of water. And it is swift and strong, all the way from the mountains.

New Zealand's longest river is the Waikato, also navigable for small boats, and also rarely navigated. The only river still navigated to any extent is the Wanganui, which winds through pastoral country, native bushland, past Maori settlements; the paddle steamer and houseboat trips up and downstream have been discontinued, and the best a tourist can now do is to take a jet-boat trip a few kilo-metres upstream from Taumaranui.

Jet-boat trips are also available on Canterbury's Waimakariri, in the South Island. Indeed, the jet-boat is a Canterbury invention, and a necessity for people who wish to navigate those great tangles of waterways where the maximum allowable draught is apt to be about one and a half centimetres. There is much deep water in the Waimakariri, particularly in the Waimakariri Gorge, where the river emerges from the high country and rushes between restricting rock walls and past pockets of native bush and small, sandy beaches; and it is this part of the trip which makes it worthwhile, for the initial stages consist of a series of twisting runs over shallow rapids, between gorse-crowned shingle banks —a noisy and rather dull proceeding, perhaps even a little alarming for people who are not

Clinton Canyon, Milford Track ▶

Clinton Canyon is a narrow, rock-walled defile through which you climb up to Mackinnon Pass, past the exquisite Lake Mintaro, fed by the mad Clinton River which rushes down from its 395 metre-high source over a short twenty-two kilometre run.

Ocean Peak and Mount Emily ▼

used to speeding through puddle-deep water.

New Zealand's lakes offer the best inland boating. Taupo, as has been described, is an inland sea, over 500 square kilometres of usually placid water which can, however, whip up on occasion to a dangerous turbulence. Willow-lined and hill-girt, its beaches strewn with pumice, (that curious, floating volcanic stone), its water temperate enough for comfortable and enjoyable swimming, teeming with trout, lying within easy reach of all the more interesting geothermal areas, it tends to be both a tourist mecca and a favourite holiday spot for New Zealanders themselves. In some areas, this attraction for the domestic holiday-makers can be a drawback, because the landscape tends to become dotted with ill-designed, jerry-built holiday houses. Taupo stood in some danger of this towards the end of the 1940s, when increasing affluence and improved roads placed it within the reach of many more people than had hitherto been the case; but intelligent town planning and careful control ensured that holiday and residential development did not spoil the sylvan beauty of the lake's shores.

The same sort of control has been applied too late to some of the southern lakes, those broad, mountain-walled, wandering sheets of water, 200 to 250 square kilometres in area, 300 metres deep, the remnants of Ice Age glaciers trapped where the ice sheet receded. Typical of these, and perhaps the most beautiful, is Wakatipu (properly Wakatipua, 'the Trench of the Demon'), at the centre point of which is Queenstown, a tiny alpine village which still retains considerable charm. There are settlements of scruffy baches here and there, while the best of the original buildings are being swept away, and the most incongruous modern styles appearing in the form of holiday houses and motels. But the lake itself, and its mountain surroundings, are breathtakingly beautiful and almost unspoilable. To look across the Frankton Arm at the Remarkables on a clear night when the snow on those striated faces reflects the moonlight, or

Bottom, snow-laden trees

The maze of ridges from which the great central peaks of the Southern Alps rise are clothed, at their lower altitudes, with native beech forest. There are, however, highland areas where there is little or no native growth, and here, man-made forests and shelter belts of hardy northern hemisphere conifers, firm the crumbling slopes. These firs thrive in areas where snow covers the ground for six months of the year, and incidentally lend to New Zealand ski slopes a flavour of Switzerland.

Top: Coronet Peak Ski Huts and Car Park

Coronet Peak is one of the venues for major ski sports competitions in New Zealand, (the other being Ruapehu, in the North Island) and the excellent, clear slopes, covered with snow for seven or eight months in a good year, attract skiers from all over the world.

Mackinnon Pass and Mount Balloon, Milford Track ▶

Billed with some justification as the most famous walk in the world, the Milford Track winds through the mountains from the head of Lake Te Anau. The way takes the tramper through the awesome Clinton Canyon and up over the Pass beneath some of the country's most stupendous peaks. The walk takes three days, with overnight stops at Pompolona and Quintin Huts, and brings you to Milford Sound.

Pyramid Hills, Lindis ▼

Brown, desert-like countryside encloses the Lindis Pass, where a road runs through from Queenstown and the Southern Lakes to the Mackenzie Basin. For all its brown, burnt appearance, and its snows in winter and fierce heat in summer, it is productive sheep country.

Opposite left: Lake Taupo Sunrise

Across Lake Taupo's 616 square kilometres, the three volcanoes of Tongariro National Park rise up above a scarf of early morning mist, and a cirrus sky promises a glorious day. Taupo abounds in trout, and this is one of its principal attractions for holiday makers.

Glendhu Bluff and Diamond Lake ▼

Glowering over Glendhu Bay on Lake Wanaka, Glendhu Bluff is a terraced, hummocky hill, in a fold in one of whose terraces is Diamond Lake, a still, mirror-like mere in a golden-brown, forest-patched fastness, a miniature of Lake Wanaka itself, overhung by the gargantuan Cosmos Peaks.

Opposite right: Remarkables, Sunset

The rugged faces of the Remarkables Range are a favourite subject for painters. Throughout the day, they present a fascinating interplay of light and shadow and changing colours; and as the sun begins to disappear behind the bulk of Queenstown's western mountain wall, and the shadow climbs up the Remarkables, the last rays of sunlight paint the jagged rocks in delicate shades of pink, against a darkening eastern sky.

to stroll through the streets at the top of the ancient terminal moraine on which the town is built, and feel the frost already in the air of an autumn afternoon when the sun has gone down behind the mountains, and the smoke from the chimneys clings to the steep, pine-covered hill, and the hawthorn and briar hips glow red-hot against the tinted hedges, is an experience which fills the mind with quiet. One is apt to forget that such peaceful, sublime beauty still exists in a raucous world.

Like the rivers and the mountains, the lakes of New Zealand vary widely in character. Within a stone's throw of Lake Wakatipu is Lake Hayes, a willow-bordered water which could have been lifted bodily, complete with the hills immediately surrounding it, from England's Lake District; within a day's easy driving, there is Wanaka, to the north, with its pleasant beaches, its brown hills and enchanting vistas of distant, snowy peaks; and to the south, Te Anau, with its deep fiords, its cave-pierced mountains; and Manapouri, forest-wrapped and dotted with forested islands.

New Zealand's mountain chains have divided the country into clearly definable areas, whose people possess certain characteristics and particular outlooks.

The Southern Alps for many years kept the people of Westland virtually isolated from the rest of the country. Westland was originally settled by miners, seeking gold initially and finding it in reasonably large quantities, and mining for coal latterly. Denied ready contact with the solid Church of England settlers of Canterbury, they became a self-sufficient people. West Coasters are a friendly,

Remarkables and Kawarau River

Leaning back from the centre reach of Lake Wakatipu, in the southern mountains, the Remarkables Range is typical of Central Otago high country. There is no softness, no tree-clad gentleness about these mountains. Here the bare rock ribs of the land are exposed, harsh and jagged. But on a moonlit night, the snow casts a reflected light over the lake; and when the late afternoon sun slants down, in the moments before it sinks behind the ranges, the tops of the Remarkables are tinged with rose pink, turning slowly to coldly-beautiful shadings and touches of blue.

open-handed people, apt to be rough in manner and speech. Yet they are, as often as not, an erudite people, placing a high value on education, both for the nourishment of the mind, (particularly important in a situation where the only diversion or entertainment available was that which they made for themselves), and for the acquisition of the kind of knowledge which enabled them to tame and control their wild environment.

The high-country people of the South Island, whatever their antecedents, are true highlanders. It would be impossible to live amongst those towering peaks, and through those white winters and burning summers without gaining an immense self-sufficiency coupled with a humility born of an overwhelming sense of one's relative size in the scheme of things. High-country people are independent, and readily acknowledge it. In powerful country, you have to know someone very well indeed before you rely on him to any vital extent, and therefore they do not readily admit outsiders into their close fellowship. Not that they are taciturn or unfriendly, as a general rule: they seem to have the gift of quietness without being sombre.

Mirror Lakes and Mount Eglinton ▲

The Mirror Lakes are small pools on the side of the road which runs from Lake Te Anau to Milford Sound. Still and sheltered, they reflect the surrounding mountains like polished glass. Mount Eglinton, and indeed, all the peaks in this area, are at their most beautiful after rain, when they are laced with hundreds of waterfalls, most of which disappear after a couple of hours of dry weather.

◀ *The Fox Glacier*

The sixteen-kilometre Fox Glacier descends on the western side of the Main Divide, from shelves of perpetual snow to gorgeously-forested hills. On the banks of the Fox River, which emerges from an ice cave at the terminal face of the glacier, are hot springs which trickle over moraine gravel to join the chill, smoky-coloured melt-water.

Queenstown from Skyline ▲

Town Hill, as the great hump which looms over the little town is prosaically named, is surmounted by the Skyline Chalet, a restaurant, access to which is by way of a cableway. From this lofty eyrie, a glorious view is obtained of the great Lake Wakatipu, the Remarkables Range, and, right underfoot, tiny Queenstown, with its narrow streets, its enchanting Gardens on the peninsula across Town Bay, and its 'suburb' of Kelvin Heights, on the bush-clad promontory in the middle distance.

Tree Ferns and Bush, Coromandel ▶

Typical of northern rain forest, this scene is one of almost tropical luxuriance. The tree ferns grow prolifically throughout most of the country, the tallest species attaining heights of around ten metres. Their lighter green fronds contrast gently with the overall dark, olive-green foliage of the forest, and the splashes of scarlet *rata*.

Lake Tarawera ▼

'Tarawera' means 'the Hot Peak', and the name was originally that of a nearby mountain, which exploded with titanic force on 10 June 1886, and threw hot rocks and ash all over the surrounding countryside, burying a small tourist village near the lake itself. Lake Tarawera is now a still and beautiful water, lapping the feet of the riven mountain. Spectacular native bush comes right down to its edge, standing back here and there to make room for a narrow curve of sandy beach. There are ancient Maori rock paintings on the Te Wairoa (Buried Village) shore, and Buried Village itself has been partially excavated.

Autumn, Lake Wanaka ▶

The wider areas, the stretches of country which are veined with close networks of roads, produce people who, if they have local characteristics, soon lose them. It is still true that people in Auckland are generally akin to Australians in outlook and accent, and that the people of Invercargill, in the deep south, are generally Scottish in attitude and speech. But these differences are not as sharply defined as they were even twenty years ago. There is a shading. The hills, which used to isolate settlements, have been tamed by good, high-speed roads. The new affluence of the second half of the twentieth century has given people more leisure for travelling, and has given a feeling of security which enables them to pack up and move about the country, confident there will always be work and somewhere to live when they arrive at their destination. So New Zealanders in these areas are a restless people, moving where the work is, not forming strong attachments to any locality—at least not to the extent of yearning to stay in it or return to it.

But there are still barriers. The man who grew up in the limestone hills of Hawkes Bay probably prefers that country to the flatness and, to him, monotony of the Canterbury Plains; but he does not find life there so very different, nor the people so very dissimilar, to those he knew in his home province. But the low-country man or the plainsman finds alpine country too hard, and the cruel peaks leaning over him too oppressive, and rarely settles in the highlands.

The Central Otago man conceives a great love for his brown land with its numbing winter frosts and its desert heat in summer. Those dry, rock-ribbed hills, with the harrier hawks wheeling on the updraughts of heated valley air, and the little green hollows with friendly stone houses and shivering poplars which occasionally delight the eye in that vastness, lay hold upon him. He is, or tends to be, a man with a gift for silences, sharing that characteristic with the high-country man. Both are hospitable, gregarious within their own environment and amongst their own people, just as the Westlanders are. And, somehow, everyone else is an outsider, in spite of the courtesy and friendliness they'll show him.

Lake Moeraki ▲

Lake Moeraki is southernmost of the exquisite South Westland lakes. Framed in bush, abounding in trout, and overlooked by the Thomas Range, it is really a broadening of the Moeraki River, six and a half square kilometres in area, and about four and a quarter metres deep at its deepest point. The surrounding forest is the haunt of deer and wild pig, and in the trees at the lake's edge may sometimes be seen *kotuku*, the Sacred White Heron. Moeraki derives its name from a type of potato, which the lake is supposed to resemble in shape.

Whangarei Falls and Forest, Northland

There is none of the awe-inspiring, brutal power possessed by many New Zealand falls to be seen in the Whangarei Falls. They are memorable for the delicate, veil-like quality of the draped water, and the sylvan loveliness of the setting. The stratification of the rock hints at titanic forces in an agonized volcanic past; but the gentle moss and shading bush, and the veil of water soothe away the last whisper of ancient fire and hurt. The Whangarei Falls are typical of Northland, where all the features found in the rest of New Zealand are reproduced on a smaller, more manageable scale.

Lake Matheson, Westland ◀

Close to the terminal face of the Fox Glacier, Lake Matheson represents the glacier's farthest reach, before a warming climate forced it to retreat back to the foot of the mountains. The lake is the melted remains of a huge block of dead ice. Surrounded by exquisite native bush, sheltered from the wind, its surface is mirror-like, and acoustics in that still area are such as to give the bird-song from the surrounding forest a quality of unearthly beauty.

Lake Hayes ▼

Lake Hayes is a small lake set in scenes of pastoral beauty, an almost surprising phenomenon so close to the vertical and harshly alpine landscape of Wakatipu, which is a mere stone's throw away. Lake Hayes is so abundant in trout that the fishing season is from October till the end of August, with an enormous limit bag. The locality is at its most beautiful in autumn, (end of March, first half of April), when the early frosts are turning the leaves of the poplars a bright yellow, and the hawthorn hedges are aglow with berries.

Papakorito Falls, Lake Waikaremoana ▶

Lake Waikaremoana, in the Urewera Highlands, is a gem of other-worldly beauty. Formed in no very remote period by the collapse of a hillside and the consequent blocking of a river valley, it spreads, blue and island-dotted, over some fifty-three square kilometres. It is fed by streams which drain nearly 340 square kilometres of densely wooded, rugged country, streams which leap down mountainsides in a series of exquisite cascades. Papakorito Falls are near a track known as the Old Gisborne Road. Some fifteen metres in height, they form lacy tiers, spreading out in a smooth flare before plunging into the basin at the foot of the three-stepped bluff.

Huka Falls, Waikato River ▶

The Huka Falls are noted, not for their height, for they are by no means lofty, but for the savage power of their green, foaming water. Viewpoints have been established along the eastern bank, securely railed, and are reached by means of a suspension bridge which crosses the river close to the actual cataract.

It is the mountains that make these people different. It is as though mountains are the only real barriers, the only features which have that property of fencing people in, and allowing them to develop independently.

New Zealand's mountain regions are inhabited; not in the way that the Swiss Alps are inhabited, or the slopes of Vesuvius, or even the American Ozarks. They are sparsely inhabited by hunters, who cull the forest-damaging deer, spending the greater part of their working lives in the steep bush. They are inhabited by the people who run mountain resorts, and who guide, and who teach climbers and skiers; but almost every New Zealander spends some time in them. They can come to grips with the mountains, living for a day or two in the shade of their stupendous peaks and shadowy gorges, tramping around their still tarns and trudging up long ridges. They can climb to the tops of the glaciers—the Tasman, the Murchison, the Fox which curves upwards into the snowy plateaux on the western side of the Alps, and the Franz Josef which, like the Fox, descends from snowfields to terminate in native bush of sub-tropical luxuriance.

Many New Zealanders, and many visitors, climb the Alps, and ski on fields like Coronet Peak, near Queenstown, or the slopes of

Ruapehu and Egmont. There are smaller fields with more primitive facilities, such as the Tararua skifield in the North Island's Wairarapa, north-east of Wellington, and Powdersnow Valley, cradled high on the flank of Mount Potts, at Erewhon, not two hours' drive from Christchurch.

The fact is that few New Zealanders live out of sight of snow-capped ranges, or out of reach of vast lakes and clean rivers. These things are commonplace, the New Zealander's heritage. He accepts them casually, and regards them as a prized but permanent possession.

Lake Middleton, Ohau

Lake Middleton is a typical high-country lake, as distinct from those trapped glacial lakes in the midst of the mountains. They are of two kinds—snow-fed and rain-fed—distinguishable from each other by their colour. (Snow-fed lakes appear from the air as lapis-lazuli blue, somewhat opaque, whereas rain-fed lakes are green-clear). The surrounding country is characteristic of the Mackenzie Basin, with its brown snowgrass, its briars and spiny *matagouri* scrub, and its clumps of dark pines, splashed in autumn with the yellow of larch.

Arrowtown Avenue

Arrowtown is one of the few gold-rush settlements which have changed very little over the years, and which are still lived in. There are new houses here, and a new pub, but many of the houses, standing back behind the trees in avenues such as this, are original miners' cottages, updated only in the matter of internal plumbing, heating arrangements and electricity.

Glendhu Bay ▼

Glendhu Bay, on Lake Wanaka, is one of the bays from which holiday crowds swim. Even in the considerable heat of summer, however, the water is very cold, and the swimming season is apt to be short. In autumn, Glendhu Bay becomes a favourite spot for trout fishermen, who catch both brown and rainbow trout in Lake Wanaka, as well as Atlantic salmon, which grow in these waters to not much more than two and a half kilograms.

◄ Head of Lake Wakatipu, Otago

This ancient, trapped glacier is a water of
superlative beauty. In this view, the
Humboldt Mountains begin to rise on the
left, and Mount Earnslaw appears on the
right. Over the low spur where a mountain
sheep station comes down to the water, the
Dart River flows into the Lake.

*Church of the Good Shepherd, Lake ▼
Tekapo*

Lake Tekapo, eighty-three square kilometres
in area, lies at an altitude of 720 metres.
On the fringe of the Mackenzie Country, it
is a popular resort for boating, water
skiing and fishing in summer, and for
skiers in winter. The Mackenzie Country
is an alpine basin, notable for sheep-raising,
and derives its name from a sheep stealer,
who first perceived its potential in the late
1800s, and proceeded to stock it with other

men's sheep. The little stone Church of the Good Shepherd is an architectural gem, obviously belonging to its environment. It is situated on a low promontory where the Tekapo River flows out of the lake. The window over the altar is of clear glass, framing a superb view of the lake and the distant, snow-capped mountains.

Bays, harbours, cliffs and coves

For a people who ventured in open, double-hulled, ocean-going canoes across the wild Pacific, the Maoris have since shown remarkably little inclination towards ocean navigation. It isn't particularly surprising, perhaps, in view of the fact that their relatively small, pre-European population had the entire, rich country to cater for their needs. They still built superb canoes, especially the great *waka taua*, the war canoes, often over thirty metres long, marvellously carved at prow and stern. The warriors sailed down the coast in them on warlike forays, and, in one incident, carried them overland, from lake to lake, finally launching them on Lake Rotorua, right in the centre of the North Island, and attacking the local tribe in their Mokoia Island stronghold. But, by and large, they did their travelling on foot, moving overland.

The European settlers, on the other hand, sailed up and down the coasts incessantly. The sea was their best method of communication in the days when every settlement was virtually isolated by dense forest and frequently threatened by hostile Maoris.

Consequently, the rugged New Zealand coasts were well charted from the earliest days of settlement.

As the charts reveal, New Zealand coastal waters can be deceptive. Northland harbours, seen from the open sea as broad, landlocked expanses of calm water, turn out to be shallow, mangrove-fringed stretches of tidal lagoon, with perhaps one medium-draught channel snaking through them. Banks Peninsula, and other deeply indented coastlines, are notched with bays that look exactly like nearby harbour entrances, and are in consequence and with grim humour, named Taylor's Mistake, Murray's Mistake and after a good many other mariners' errors and tragic misjudgments.

But much of the coastline is well provided with deep bays and landlocked coves which make the country a small-boatman's dream.

Types of coastal scenery vary widely, even over a comparatively short length of coast. Within the Bay of Islands, for example, there are golden-sand beaches, gravel beaches, mangrove-tangled tidal mud flats, *pohutukawa*-splashed bush standing directly over the water, huge pinnacles of sea-sculpted rock and miniature estuaries.

Tauranga, 480 kilometres down the east coast from the Bay of Islands, spreads itself around a broad bay pitted with coves and sheltered by the long, low mass of Matakana Island. Many of its coves are strongly reminiscent of tropical isles, with their golden-sand beaches and spits, and white pleasure-craft riding serenely in the shade of palm-like treeferns.

There are drab, grey shingle beaches, such as those which lie along the Napier foreshore, swept by strong currents, steeply shelving and dangerous; or south of Banks Peninsula, at Birdlings Flat, where the fierce rip has torn at the volcanic cliffs and deposited gemstones profusely along the steep and perilous shingle bank which separates Lake Ellesmere from the Pacific Ocean.

Some of the world's finest seascapes are to be found in New Zealand, such as the glorious view from Florence Hill, in the Catlins District of South Otago, where a vast sweep of forest-fringed beach ends where the green and delightful Tautuku Peninsula thrusts out into the empty sea.

Mahurangi Peninsula, North Auckland

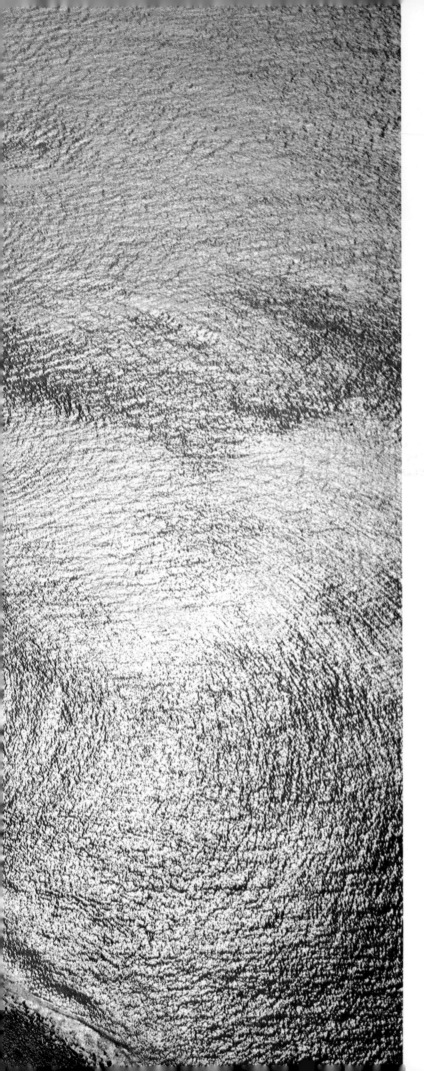

In the south-west are the fiords, drowned glacial valleys cutting far into the mountainous bulk of the land, walled by peaks which climb vertically to the sky from the water's edge, or by gentler but still steep slopes clad in dark, untrodden forest where the mornings are greeted by the chiming of a million bellbirds.

On the western side of the North Island, the great, carved bluffs of Tongaporutu, bush-crowned and frowning, give way gradually to the black ironsand beaches of northern Taranaki, backed by steep gulley-riven slopes, a stern landscape, seen from the sea, but full of bush-clad, bird-haunted beauty, over which Mount Egmont broods silently; and southern Taranaki, flat beyond the hem of Egmont's spreading skirts, lies clifftop-high above buff-coloured sand and sea-gnawed caves.

North-west of Wellington, fine beaches, protected from the rages of the temperamental Tasman Sea by Kapiti and Mana Islands, are interspersed with jagged reefs and bastions of rock; but the beaches narrow perceptibly and the reefs are more frequent as they near Cape Terawhiti at the butt-end of a range of mountainous ridges which drop down abruptly to the turbulent and wind-whipped Cook Strait.

Those rugged ranges once stretched all the way across to Marlborough, in what is now the South Island; but some cataclysmic subsidence snapped the chain at its northern end and dragged the Marlborough mountains down beneath the sea.

Cape Kidnappers Gannet Colony

Lying like the tail of a dragon in a patch of turbulent sea, Cape Kidnappers holds, on a flat and slightly sloping hump, a gannet colony of some 2 800 pairs of these graceful birds, which look like a cross between a pelican and a goose. There are actually two nesting sites, the one shown being accessible to visitors by way of a razor-backed path with steep and rather perilous slopes dropping away on either side.

Their drowned valleys are now magnificent waterways, where high, densely-forested peninsulas and islands organize the sea into a complex of bays and straits, sheltered, deep and teeming with fish. Known as Marlborough Sounds, they reach far inland, the longest arm lapping the feet of the small town of Havelock, and their secluded bays enfolding holiday baches, occasional homes, farms, hotels and guest houses. The beaches, built up over aeons of time, are sometimes sandy, more often golden gravel. The bush echoes all day to the chime of *tui* and bellbirds, and *ruru*, the little bush owl, calls across the glinting water at night.

Westland shores are swept in places by a warm ocean current which, with the sunshine, warms the air between the high Alps and the sea, and produces luxuriant forest, and at least one sandy beach where the tall *nikau* palms add to the tropical aspect of the place. Other Westland beaches are wild and lonely stretches of driftwood-strewn granite sand, reaching around swampy lagoons such as Okarito, where the white heron nests.

New Zealand abounds in good harbours. Auckland's Waitemata is wide and deep, a vast inreaching from the Hauraki Gulf, where the sea wanders up long reaches to mingle with tidal creeks. Its mouth is shielded by the broad, flat cone of Rangitoto, and it is separated from the shallower Manukau by the slim Tamaki Isthmus. Mangroves grow in its shallower arms, and the occasional small, rocky reef and island breaks its sparkling surface. It is a pond-like harbour, mostly, with the land gently sloping down into it— a shallow, drowned valley.

Wellington Harbour, though, is a perfectly land-locked basin, surrounded by high hills. Captain Herd of the barque *Rosanna* wrote in the *Nautical Almanac*, around 1826, that '. . . here all the navies of Europe might ride in perfect security'.

Lyttelton Harbour, on the northern side of Banks Peninsula, is a long rift, an open-sided crater of a volcanic explosion which would have dwarfed the biggest nuclear bomb yet devised. It is entered through high, embrasured cliffs, where once the guns of shore batteries were emplaced in an antipodean Gibraltar, which now houses seabirds and pigeons. The town of Lyttelton clambers up the inside of the crater wall, flanked by bush-filled fissures and frowned upon by the blasted lava at the rim.

Mitre Peak ▲

Milford Sound is one of the drowned glacial valleys which deeply notch the South Westland coast of the South Island. Deep, bottle-green water and titanic rock walls and forested cliffs rising sheer from the water to heights of 1 500 metres make sailing in these waters an unforgettable experience. Mitre Peak, centre, is one of the highest peaks rising straight out of the water anywhere in the world.

◄ Mount Maunganui

The Mount, as it is affectionately known, is a long, curving beach near Tauranga, in the Bay of Plenty, terminating in a lofty, conical peak, the site of ancient Maori fortifications. The beach is a much favoured venue for competitive surfing.

◀ Coromandel Peninsula

The Coromandel Peninsula forms the eastern bastion which shelters the Hauraki Gulf. Hilly and partly forested, its deeply indented shores today provide a number of delightful holiday resorts, golden sand beaches, sheltered and breathtakingly lovely. Coromandel was the scene of a gold strike in 1867, when a reef was discovered which paid handsomely for almost 100 years.

Punakaiki Pancake Rocks ▼

One of Westland's finest beaches, Punakaiki is caressed by a warm ocean current, and the *nikau* palms, the lush, sub-tropical bush which clothes the backdrop of steep ranges, and the smooth sand, make it a favourite and increasingly sought-after holiday place for New Zealanders. The Pancake Rocks are a peculiar geological feature. With the distinct appearance of piles of pancakes, they are pierced by blowholes, through which the inrushing sea fountains upwards, geyser-like, with much subterranean rumbling and sighing.

Opposite: Cape Reinga, Northland

According to Maori lore, Cape Reinga, at the extreme north of the North Island, is the departing place for the spirits of the dead. Here the Tasman Sea and the Pacific ocean meet, in a fierce striving of opposing currents. The sea is a deep blue, shading off to pastel greens near the shore and stitched with lines of white breakers on the reefs. The Maoris say that when a vessel sinks in these seas, a rainbow marks the spot.

Opposite right: Whangaroa Harbour

Whangaroa is typical of Northland's shallow, mangrove-fringed harbours. It winds and twists between high hills, and is looked down upon by two massive rock domes, one on either side, called St Peter's and St Paul's Cupolas. A favourite holiday spot, the Whangaroa provides fine boating water and good fishing.

Opposite left: Hicks Bay, Poverty Bay

Poverty Bay was so named by Captain James Cook because he was unable to obtain either provisions or friendliness from the Maoris in the area, in marked contrast to his reception at the Bay of Plenty, to the north of East Cape.

Moeraki Boulders, Otago

Moeraki Beach is named after the potato which ancient Polynesian voyagers brought with them in their great double-hulled, ocean-going canoe. The canoe, so the olden legend goes, capsized near Shag Point, at the end of the beach, and the *moeraki* potatoes and some gourds which she was carrying were strewn by the tide along the beach, and were later transformed into boulders. Today, these septarian stones lie half buried in sand, a geological oddity, rusty-red or yellow inside, with crystalline cores.

Cape Brett ▼

Cape Brett is the eastern head at the entrance to the Bay of Islands. Hereabouts is a famous big game fishing ground, and the famous Hole in the Rock which is one of the features of special launch cruises, which take passengers through the Hole and into the Grand Cathedral Cave in the vicinity.

The port complex is behind man-made breakwaters and moles, for the prevailing north-east wind comes up the harbour with funnelled force, and its open water can be very rough. The cliffs and bays around the harbour are dotted with pleasant settlements, and the crater itself is old and eroded now, filled at the southern end with the hills and humps formed by the debris of centuries, all grassy and tree-grown.

On the southern side of the peninsula, Akaroa Harbour is similar, but smaller and shallower, with the one-time French settlement of Akaroa clinging to such flat harbour-side land as can be found, and wandering up valleys which trend away from the sea, still sentimentally calling its streets Rue Viard and Rue Balguerie and still carefully preserving its quaint French houses with their lacy wrought-iron balconies and their elegant doors and windows.

At the mouth of Akaroa Harbour, and around the north-eastern corner of the peninsula, red volcanic cliffs lean out over the heaving sea, pitted with small caves, the bubbles of the once boiling lava perhaps, or the mouths of fumaroles. Now they are nesting places for shags.

Dunedin Harbour is long and narrow, like Lyttelton, but shallower. The deepest water is at Port Chalmers, near the mouth, a Lyttelton-like town that clambers up the steep hillsides from the water's edge; but a painstakingly dredged channel, carefully marked with buoys and pylons, snakes up to Dunedin itself.

The eastern side of the harbour is the Otago Peninsula. On its ocean shore, there are bays where the kelp swirls around barnacled rocks, and seals bask on offshore islets; and there are sandy inlets with bush-fringed beaches, and caverns where the sea surges in and out and sends strange boomings up deep fissures to the grassy hillsides above. And over all of this enchanting coastline, the ancient lava plugs look down from the hilltops of a timeless sort of land where farms still have drystone fences, and there are houses of grey local stone, and even a castle, the famous Larnach's, from which its builder could spy trading ships approaching the harbour, whereupon he would make haste to have his agents down on the wharf, the first to meet them and the first to pick over their cargoes.

Just as few New Zealanders live out of sight of snow-capped mountain ranges, none lives more than two or three hours' drive from the coast. Beaches, harbours and coves are easily accessible, which is why a boat-building business can thrive in a centre like Fairlie or Taumaranui, which are about as far inland as it is possible to get. New Zealanders are, generally speaking, boating enthusiasts. They are small-boat people, knowledgeable about their home waters, weatherwise because in an island climate they have to be, and bold, resourceful sailors.

After all, their small-boat tradition goes back a long way, to those missionaries who pottered around uncharted coasts; to the sealers and whalers who felt their way into and out of strange bays and uninhabited fiords, to the Maoris from the Bay of Plenty, who farmed and gardened land in Northland in the early 1800s and traded their produce down the coast in their own fleet of small schooners; and the crayfishers along the Kaikoura Coast today, who nose their craft in and out of some impossibly narrow, monstrously turbulent gut in a kelp-draped, swirl-washed reef, and winch it up at day's end to some shelf which the highest tides and stormiest seas won't reach.

Standing on a bleak spot of the Wairarapa coast, the lighthouse protects shipping from the huge seas that pound the cliffs.

One of the country's most celebrated beaches, Kaiteriteri is a broad crescent of coarse golden sand, sheltered at either end by bush-crowned promontories. Azure water and the drab olive green of beech, with gums and pines standing along the crest of each headland, and the reddish gold of the beach, make it one of the most photogenic beaches. Facing into Golden Bay, and thus protected from the wild winds of the Tasman, it lies as a kind of backwater, by-passed by the swift current of Cook Strait, calm, safe and greatly favoured for boating and swimming, the perfect holiday beach.

◀ *Kaikoura*

Kaikoura received its name from an ancient Maori explorer, who caught *koura*, the crayfish, here, and enjoyed a meal of it. The name means 'feast of crayfish'. The present-day town is tucked into the foot of the peninsula, where it joins the mainland, and is backed by the magnificent Seaward Kaikoura Range. In this view, showing a reef near the tip of the peninsula in the foreground and the town in its picturesque setting, the sea is in one of its calmer moods, a flat calm with a steely-blue tint to the water. More commonly, in winter, the nor'-east winds whip it into a frenzy, causing great breakers to crash in dense clouds of spume and spray along the rocky coast.

Gog and Magog, Stewart Island ▶

Stewart Island, a mountainous island of some 1 700 square kilometres, separated from the southern end of the South Island by one of the roughest stretches of water in the New Zealand territory, is sparsely inhabited, most of the inhabitants being fishermen and their families. It has one township, Oban, beautifully situated in a forest-girt bay. Stewart Island's coastline is rugged, but it possesses beaches and coves of Eden-like beauty, golden sand alternating with silvery sand, often strewn with a scarlet seaweed.

Sandy Bay, Otago ▼

Here the force of the wave patterns of the Great Southern Ocean are deeper felt than any other part of New Zealand. The clear blue water is intensely cold.

There is no such thing as a large commercial fishing fleet in New Zealand, no equivalent of those enormous Japanese trawlers and factory ships which cross the Pacific to fish out a hundred shores. New Zealand commercial fishermen have always fished comparatively close inshore, taking what they need and rather deploring the kind of enterprise which strips a productive area bare.

Fish are becoming hard to find; yet sporting fishermen still make good catches off northern beaches, such as Bayly's Beach, near Dargaville, where local fishermen use a raft, floated out from the beach, laden with baited hooks. They call it a 'galloping gertie'. Birdlings Flat fishermen, in the South Island, use a similar device, called a Kon Tiki, to catch snapper and blue cod.

At the mouths of Canterbury's great rivers, salmon are caught, in season. Anglers often stand a metre or two apart along a tide-and-current-built spit of sand. And on some northern beaches, notably Ninety Mile Beach, (which is actually about half that length), the flat, smooth-washed strip of clean sand backed by the dunes and dune-like hills of the Aupori Peninsula, the *toheroa* is obtained, a large, clam-like shellfish with a flavour as delicate as, but nothing resembling, the finest oysters. *Toheroas*, which make a delicious green soup often favourably compared with turtle soup, are found in only a few localities, and there is a strict limit to the numbers which people may take. In less favoured areas, they make do with the *pipi*, another, smaller clam-like creature which is nevertheless delicious, boiled and eaten with bread and butter and vinegar.

Few districts are not within reach of good surfing and swimming beaches, seashores like Pourerere, in Central Hawkes Bay, where there is more than a kilometre of sandy bottom and huge, crashing Pacific rollers, tamed sufficiently by the broad continental shelf to be safe, powerful enough to provide a thrilling ride shorewards; and there are areas of swimming-pool still water, sheltered by grey *papa* reefs, some of which, completely uncovered at low tide, are veritable marine gardens, their rock pools alive with all manner of fascinating life.

Indeed, there is a great wealth of accessible golden-sand beaches, like those glorious curves backed by steep, forested hills, along the South Otago coast. The water is apt to be cold—a steady 15°C winter and summer—but it teems with fish; and those hills immediately behind the beaches are laced with tumbling forest brooks and waterfalls and lakelets of sublime loveliness. And they're empty, most of those beaches. Their caves, their tall cliffs stratified interestingly with rock and coal, their bared scarps of volcanic conglomerate which looks as crumbly as cheese but is actually hard as ferro-concrete and contains microscopic sapphires and emeralds, products of the fiery alchemy of the world's birth, are visited spasmodically but never crowded. There are beaches to spare.

And they teem with a variety of life, offshore. The Bay of Islands has its big game fish, the swordfish and the marlin.

Off Kaikoura, seals swim, and whales are not uncommonly observed as they surface briefly and blow; and on the ocean side of the Otago Peninsula, there are beaches where, punctually in the early evening, hordes of penguins surf into the beach, waddle ashore, preen shining wet feathers, and disappear into the tussock and scrub above the beach, to nest for the night.

Queen Charlotte Sound

The network of drowned valleys which form the Marlborough Sounds are poems of placid, deep water and forested peninsulas. Queen Charlotte Sound, with the township and entry-port of Picton at its head, is the busiest, with fishing boats, pleasure craft and the inter-island rail-ferries, *Aramoana* and *Aranui*, plying from the Picton harbour; launch traffic, fishing and carrying supplies and mail for outlying farms, finds its way into all of the waterways.

Cities in search of the best of two worlds

Until recently, there has been very little difference between New Zealand cities and New Zealand small towns, except for the size of the populations. Perhaps the cities have possessed buildings which run to seven or eight storeys, whereas two is about the limit for small towns; but New Zealanders have always been uneasy when deprived of green grass and growing plants, and have clung resolutely to the quarter-acre building section.

Streets and streets of bungalows, usually wooden, mostly single-storeyed, have spread out around a commercial centre with one or more streets of shops and blocks of office buildings; and the inhabitants usually came to the city centre at least once a week to 'do the shops'.

Life in a city has always been, until quite recently, precisely like life in a country town, with the addition of a bus service and a few more theatres, pubs and places of entertainment.

But the change is happening, and happening fast. Across the isthmus of the northern peninsula, lumpy with its ancient volcanic cones, Auckland spreads like a many-coloured cloth. Most cosmopolitan of New Zealand cities, and the largest, (pop. 500 000-plus), Auckland is a lively, bustling place. It still sprawls, and always will, a vast conglomeration of multi-coloured houses. But high-rise buildings are springing up like mushrooms in tight clusters in the city's commercial heart, and new shopping complexes and malls are growing in suburbs which, ten or fifteen years ago, were satellite towns. People in suburbs like Three Kings or Papatoetoe, now inseparably part of Auck-

land proper, still shop and live within their own boundaries, just as they always did, because it simply isn't worth while to go across the busy town to the central Queen Street and Karangahape Road areas.

Auckland crowds down to the small, sandy bays of the Waitemata (Sparkling Waters) harbour, which, many branched, serves as the Aucklanders' almost universal playground. The harbour influences their lifestyle profoundly, making of them an outdoor people. It could hardly be otherwise, for they see it every day. Thousands of them cross it, driving or riding in buses over the great Auckland Harbour Bridge, coming from North Shore suburbs to work in the city centre. Their preferred suburbs and dwelling areas are within sight and easy reach of it. Everyone's ambition is to own a boat of some kind, and to sail on its broad, uncluttered surface.

For it is a superb boating harbour, big enough not to be too crowded with the shipping of commerce, sheltered by Rangitoto and, farther out on the Hauraki Gulf, Waiheke Island's larger bulk, and protected from the madder moods of the Pacific Ocean by the long finger of Coromandel Peninsula and the huge hump of Great Barrier Island.

New Zealanders generally tend to believe that Auckland is the place where it's all happening; and indeed, there are theatres, raceways, sportsgrounds, a sub-tropical climate, (bananas grow in Auckland), and an overall impression of a loud and colourful life.

If Auckland sprawls leisurely about her wandering harbour, Wellington crowds closely about hers, leaning over it, dabbling her toes in it, borrowing some of its ample

area on which to build her commercial centre, a seemingly precarious foothold on a few meagre acres of reclaimed land in which streets are jammed together haphazardly, and little, narrow lanes dart between close-crowded buildings.

Wellington, like Auckland, is easily accessible; by rail, by ferries from Lyttelton and Picton in the South Island, and by air. Its international airport is a minor marvel of engineering, for it juts into the harbour at one end, and into Cook Strait at the other; a whole, large, bulky hill, covered with houses, had to be removed in the course of its construction.

Wellington knew the high-rise building before Auckland did, and erected office blocks like towers—for a different reason. I suspect that Auckland's tallest buildings were always marks of her affluence and opulence, whereas Wellington's were born of necessity. For Wellington is the country's capital, and therefore the administrative centre of New Zealand. Here are the head offices of many of its biggest corporations, its insurance companies and its banks. All of them have to crowd on to that slim strip of reclaimed land, where the main thoroughfare still follows the curve of the original beach, and still retains the name, Lambton Quay, though it is now mostly three blocks from the wharves. Head-office buildings couldn't, therefore, spread out. They had to go upwards.

Wellington and Mount Victoria

Wellington's business and administrative heart crowds around the harbour, its growing office and hotel buildings and commercial development blocks gradually pushing out the fringe of older residential housing. The principal wharves are from centre to centre left in this view. The large wharf in the middle distance is the overseas terminal, where passengers from overseas liners disembark unencumbered by the traffic of the cargo wharves.

57

Bottom left: Boat Harbour, Oriental Bay, Wellington

Wellington harbour offers splendid boating water. Land-locked and surrounded by the city on its steep hillsides, the harbour possesses numerous sandy bays, the nearest of which to the city centre is Oriental Bay, a delightful stretch of wave-lapped sand mere minutes from the commercial heart of Wellington. The boat harbour lies between the beach and the base of the Overseas Terminal wharf.

Bottom right: Blossom and Daffodils, Hagley Park

Hagley Park is divided into two main sections, between which runs the main road from Riccarton to town. This section of the road passes through woodland, mostly English trees, with plantings of cherries and other blossom trees. In springtime, commuters on the red Christchurch buses ride in to work past these delightful glades, a blaze of green and white and gold.

Opposite top: Westhaven Sunrise, Auckland

It is the ambition of almost every Aucklander to own some sort of small boat, which is not surprising in view of the ideal conditions offered by the harbour, and the opportunities for deep-water sailing out in the Hauraki Gulf, with its many islands. Westhaven is one of a number of small-boat harbours around the shores of the Waitemata.

Opposite bottom: Southern Alps and Christchurch from Cashmere

From the hillside suburb of Cashmere, superb views are obtained of the plains and the distant mountains. The suburb seen spread across the plain in this view is Halswell, south-easternmost of the Christchurch residential areas. In the distance is Wigram Air Base, one of the birthplaces of New Zealand aviation and still a Royal New Zealand Air Force base.

Wellington has, for many years, crushed into that tiny space, with its residential sections climbing and clambering up alarming gradients on the surrounding high hills, where they still perch like seabirds on rocky platforms in the midst of unmolested patches of original bush and runaway acreages of pioneer-planted gorse.

Ultimately, the city had to break out, and the cable car, (there is just one pair, on one double track), opened up the hinterland. Land which had been lying vacant behind that first range of formidable ridges was now cleared for building. It was at last a viable proposition to build a home there, for now the city and one's place of business were mere minutes away.

Even so, westward expansion is still limited by the difficulty of building on steep, slip-prone hills, and eastward expansion is even more difficult because of the bush-clad Orongorongo Range, which rears up a stone's throw from the harbour shore. The overflow of Wellington's population of workers is now accommodated in Petone, Wellington's twin city which begins at the harbour-head beach and spreads northwards up the Hutt Valley. Or it lives in the one-time satellite town and now virtual suburb of Johnsonville, in a fold in the hills, reached by the Ngauranga Gorge, or by a railway which darts in and out of the tunnels which pierce the granite hills. More still are housed in the dormitory city of Porirua, thirty odd kilometres up the north-west coast. Wellington proper, therefore, is unlikely to grow much bigger in terms of area, which makes it a manageable, pleasant city to live in.

By and large, it is not a city of quarter-acre sections with well-tended gardens, because the nature of the terrain precludes any such arrangement over much of its area. But it is something which is perhaps more beautiful. Once you get out of the city centre and into the suburbs—Kelburn and Karori in particular—you find yourself in a city-in-a-forest. Steep sections are still thick with original growth of native bush, with long flights of steps leading up from the streets to the half-hidden houses. Here and there, in newer and flatter suburbs, the familiar quarter-acre section with its formal garden is

Hamilton City from Hamilton Lake Domain ▼

Hamilton is an inland city, principal town of the Waikato, in the Auckland Province, and one of the fastest-growing of all New Zealand cities. Straddling the Waikato River, it is beginning to sprawl across the rich Waikato landscape. An attractive city, blessed by a mild climate, it features some beautiful residential areas bordering Hamilton Lake, tree-shaded and bird-haunted, with huge Monarch butterflies fluttering amid bright gardens.

Dunedin City and Octagon ▶

The Octagon is Dunedin's city centre. In fact, the gardened and tree-shaded area to which the name has become attached is not as true an octagon as the streets which run one block out from the centre—but the central area is nevertheless beautiful, with its Robert Burns statue, (that indispensible furnishing of any truly Scottish city), and the Gothic facade of the Anglican Cathedral standing at the head of a broad flight of steps. The Town Hall balconies look out over the Octagon, and from here historic announcements and royalty and other notables have been heard by great crowds. The area slopes gently to the sun.

apparent, a splash of contrivance in the midst of natural artlessness; but the overall impression is of tree-screened houses on hillsides.

Wellington is tending to be a city of architectural extremes—the avant-garde beside the Victorian and Edwardian; houses perched on dizzy tops and ledges overlooking homes set in delightful valleys and dells.

It's all quite unlike Christchurch, second largest city in New Zealand. Christchurch has half the population of Auckland, but sprawls over almost as great an area. Like all South Island towns, it is rather better planned than the North Island cities, because it was planned down to the finest detail by its founders before its first citizens ever set foot

in New Zealand. Maori-Pakeha relations in the South Island were generally good which made the purchase of land easier. The land on which Christchurch was built is billiard-table flat, and the immigration planning included the bringing out of sufficient artisans and labourers to implement the plan properly.

Christchurch is a four-square sort of city. Its main streets are generally wide and straight, and cross one another at precise right angles. It is said to be an 'English' city, with its Gothic Revival cathedral sited dead centre, in the city square, and its remarkable Provincial Council Chamber, relic of the days when each province had its own government, and built like a little West-

minster, its earlier portion, holding ministerial offices, in wood, and the later Council Chamber, for all the world like the House of Commons and containing the finest barrel-vaulted ceiling in the southern hemisphere, in locally quarried stone. It stood on the banks of the pretty Avon stream, when first erected, alone and splendid, surrounded by the newly formed streets and precious few other buildings, a mark of the self-confidence of the colonists.

Christchurch is beautiful, in places. Like all cities, its industrial areas are drab at best, hideously scruffy at worst; but its older residential sections, particularly in the north-western quarter, are places of gracious homes of all sizes, tree-shaded and surrounded by proud gardens and venerable oaks, elms and limes. The Avon River, flowing through the heart of the city, is bordered by smooth lawns and fine garden plots, and is bridged by a number of graceful bridges, many of them little Victorian gems, with their lace-like wrought iron railings painted a fresh white and blue.

Part of Christchurch climbs into the hills of Banks Peninsula. Here is the old-established but still growing suburb of Cashmere, with its native trees and bluegums and its maze of winding streets; or the hills overlooking the estuary of the Avon and Heathcote Rivers, and the prodigious sweep of Pegasus Bay. Houses here perch high on ledges of volcanic rock, and cliffs are draped, in summer, with red-and-purple ice plant.

Lombardy Poplars in Autumn Colour,
Avon River

The Avon, when the settlers arrived, was a swampy creek. One of their first tasks was to barber it into a pleasant, free-flowing waterway, navigable for small coastal schooners for some distance. In the course of time, the banks were gardened and trees, including these magnificent Lombardy poplars, planted. A city businessman gave, early this century, a long stretch of concrete balustrading, complete with landing stages and rings for tying up boats and punts, with a fine colonnaded bandstand, still used for Sunday night concerts, and a nearby concrete shelter. Punts have gone out of fashion, but the embankment, shaded by poplars, is still very beautiful.

Christchurch is a city of small theatres, including two very fine theatres in its new Town Hall complex. It is a place of immense parks, such as Hagley Park, with its formal gardens, its golf course, its sports grounds and its woodlands, all right in the centre of the city, and guarded zealously, not to say jealously, by Christchurch citizens. The Christchurch International Airport is the country's finest, being capable of indefinite expansion in almost any direction, for Christchurch is situated on the Canterbury Plains.

Christchurch sprawls, as Auckland does; but here the sprawl is somewhat undesirable, since the city is swallowing up fertile farmland at an alarming rate. Yet the city still possesses this charming characteristic, that you can be driving along through a densely populated area, street after street of bungalows—and, suddenly, you turn a corner, and you're in the midst of quiet farmland, where tall poplars and dark *macrocarpa* grow, and cows stand somnolently in their shade. You take another turn, and you're in the city again.

It also has the advantage of stretching along kilometres of safe, sandy beach, where the surf is good and the water sparklingly clean.

Dunedin, fourth of New Zealand's four 'main centres', is frankly Victorian. This is not to say that it is lacking in amenities of the most up-to-date kind. Indeed, it has some very fine, very modern hotels, is a centre of considerable artistic and cultural activity; but it has many substantial mansions, built and occupied at a time when many North Island centres were rude collections of *raupo* huts—and the delightful thing is that they are still occupied, in many cases, by the families whose forebears built them. Wellington's Victorian and Edwardian villas are most usually divided inside into a number of flats; but those proud old houses in Dunedin are still, more often than not, family homes.

Dunedin, like Wellington, is a city in a forest. It is possible to take winding drives around its steep hillsides, along broad streets with paved footpaths and good lighting, and see very few houses. They are there, all right, but are hidden in little, leafy islands of peace and quiet. Five minutes from the city centre, there are areas of exquisite and unspoiled beauty, a green belt which has every intention of remaining a green belt, and will probably do so for ages to come. For Dunedin is conservative in the best sense of the word. Progress for the sake of progress is not its way. There's a strong strain of good Scottish commonsense which builds where building is clearly required, and tears down where neither use nor pleasure can reasonably be expected any more.

Dunedin, like Christchurch, has its clean, sandy beaches, Ocean Grove, St Kilda and St Clare, with others on the ocean side of the Otago Peninsula reachable by some fairly precipitous roads.

Of the provincial centres, there are coastal cities like New Plymouth, Tauranga and Napier in the North Island, and inland towns such as Hamilton and Palmerston North, and, in the South Island, Blenheim and Ashburton.

Coastal cities, generally speaking, were centres of earliest European settlement. Inland cities, as might be expected, were founded much later.

Hamilton, for example, was founded around 1864, originally as two towns, both military settlements occupied by Fencibles, the 4th Waikato Regiment, an army of occupation following the expulsion of adherents of the Maori King. Each man was given 50 acres to farm, and a one-acre town section. They built redoubts on either side of the Waikato River, and the settlements that grew up around them were known as Hamilton East and Hamilton West. Eventually, of course, a substantial bridge made traffic between the two villages safer, and the two settlements became one.

Christchurch Town Hall

Opened in 1973, the Christchurch Town Hall complex has won acclaim from overseas visitors. Containing two excellent theatres, a restaurant and administrative offices, the building stands on the banks of the Avon, partially screened by venerable willows, except where the fountain plays in a pool slightly raised above the placid Avon.

Hamilton today is a rapidly growing business centre, with its university, its factories and its sprawling housing. The administrative centre of some of the richest dairying land in the world, it is a thriving, bustling place, which has managed to retain much of its beauty. The riverbank is attractively laid out, and Hamilton Lake is a tree-bordered reach of placid water where swans glide and ducks bring up large families.

New Plymouth is an older settlement—not quite a quarter of a century older. It is a seaside town, hilly and pleasant, with its older part still clinging close to the waterfront, its street pattern tending to be four-square, as befits a planned town, but with wandering ways cutting diagonally across the orderly squares, or wandering beside a brawling little stream, probably because the settlers, with some disregard for the schemes of the planners, insisted on taking the easiest path between two points rather than the direct one. Also, New Plymouth was under seige in 1860, and it is possible that some of the city's ways were the shortest paths to defence points about the perimeter. Whereas Hamilton was intended from the first as a garrison town, New Plymouth became one because of the fortunes of war. Its lovely old St Mary's stone church, with its pillars carved from whole *puriri* trees, and its brass plaques expressing gratitude for sanctuary during the troubled times, still bears around its nave the hatch-ments of many famous British regiments, and the colours of famous New Zealand regiments which were born in those times.

Life in these provincial centres is pleasant. There is not the crush and hustle of a metropolis, yet there are entertainments and cultural activities, and most of the amenities one associates with a modern western-style city. They are still undoubtedly big small-towns, with their shopping centres still confined to a specific downtown area, wherein everyone shops at least once a week; and they retain that degree of civic pride which is the mark of the small-town community. They are entities, not too big to grasp. The inhabitants, far from knowing everyone in town as can be the case in a very small town, are at least aware of everyone. And they have an identity. They are Hamilton people, or New Plymouth people. This is passing, in the larger centres. In Auckland, people tend to be North Shore people, or Devonport people, or Onehunga (pronounce it Oh-knee-hunga) people. Wellingtonians, those who live in Wellington itself, are definitely and happily Wellingtonians; but, of course, many of the people working in Wellington don't happen to live there, and many who do live there happen to have come to Wellington on transfer within their firm or department, and still regard themselves as Hastings or Waipukurau people. In Christchurch, the citizens in the older suburbs—Riccarton, Woolston, Fendalton, St Albans, Merivale, Papanui, Spreydon, Cashmere—regard themselves as Christchurch people; but people in the newer suburbs, where Christchurch has flowed out into the countryside—Bishopdale, Hornby, Halswell, Upper Riccarton—seem to be assuming an almost separate identity, and the old small-town spirit is fading.

Dunedin people, of course, are Dunedin people; but even here there is evidence that the city has become a collection of suburbs and fringe settlements.

Top: Orchards near Hastings

Poplar-lined paddocks and orchards are a familiar sight in Hawkes Bay. Hastings, the 'fruit bowl of New Zealand', is an important fruit and vegetable processing town.

◀ *Civic Square, Palmerston North*

A pleasant inland city on the Manawatu Plain, Palmerston North has become an important educational and cultural centre.

New Zealanders generally have been a small-town people with a small-town outlook and culture. It is rapidly becoming less true of them. The very smallest towns no longer seem to be regarded as places in which people are born, live their lives and die. They are, at most, dormitories. Of those who live in them, many look with some longing towards the cities, believing that there is where it is all happening. If they can't often go to the city, they still live an intensely urban life vicariously, through the media of television, radio and cinema. Many of the smallest rural communities are decaying. But the larger country towns, places like Rangiora, Waimate, Marton, Kaitaia, are still great places to live, proud of their achievements and the good life they offer. The towns are trimmed and barbered and full of community activity.

Our greatest men and women, our leaders in almost every field, have been small-town people, more often than not. I rather think that it is because of our small-town outlook and attitudes that New Zealand has often been a world leader in, for instance, some aspects of social legislation. We've never, even in our largest cities, been so big that people have become mere statistics. But—it's beginning to happen. There is room for a great many more small towns of from two to ten thousand population. I hope we build them, and refuse to allow our cities to grow any larger.

◀ *Wanganui City and River*

Wanganui is an attractive city situated five kilometres upstream from the river mouth, amidst rolling sheep and beef country.

New Plymouth and Mount Egmont ▼

New Plymouth clusters about the foreshore as if, like the original settlers, it is reluctant to push inland. New suburbs, however, are now thrusting in to the deep, bush-filled rifts and the green hillsides behind the city proper. New Plymouth has some delightful parks and public gardens, from any one of which breathtaking vistas of dark hills and the cone of Mount Egmont may be obtained through a frame of native bush.

The wilderness tamed

New Zealand has been settled, successively and at no very remote period, by three distinct types of immigrant.

The first were the Moa Hunters, arriving probably about the 10th century A.D., from Pacific islands, notably Tahiti. They made little mark on the land, and appear to have been hunter-gatherers, content to harvest the rich bounty of the sea, and to hunt the *moa*, a flightless grazing bird, the largest species of which were about the size of a large emu.

The later arrivals, who came in what is spoken of traditionally as the Great Fleet Migration, were more vigorous and considerably more aggressive. They cultivated plots of land, whereon they planted *kumara*, a type of sweet potato; yet they were, in a sense, nomadic, for they moved seasonally from cultivations to bird forest to eel weir and duck lake to the coast, within certain prescribed tribal boundaries. Their greatest land-shaping efforts were in the field of military engineering, at which they were supremely gifted. (In later clashes with Europeans, they built fortresses which were proof against the heaviest artillery of the day, and so riddled with tunnels and hidden ways that, even if the enemy did manage to enter them, large bodies of warriors could pop up in their rear, with devastating results.) Many a hilltop still shows plainly the trenching and terracing of fortified villages.

The European arrived, bent upon re-creating for himself the kind of homeland that he had left behind. He built his towns, and he worked with axe and firestick to clear vast areas of virgin forest for use as farmland. He made a considerable impression on the land, not only in the amount of it which was once bush and is now pasture, but also in the erosion he caused because he didn't understand the part that bush plays in holding hillsides firm under the seasonally heavy rainfall.

So many of the steeper tracts of hill country are today scarred by massive slips, and much formerly useful land has acquired a coat of gorse which is rather more dense and much more difficult to eradicate than it is in England, from where the first fatal seeds were imported.

But, on the credit side, the pioneer worked the land, and did it well. I have diary pages written by my grandfather in the 1860s, which are chiefly interesting for the insight which they give into the way in which farming practice changed in a relatively short period. It changed, quite clearly, from the secure, hedged-field husbandry of England, with its flocks numbered in mere hundreds, to the management of flocks numbering thousands, spread over a countryside which was steep, with swamps in its

Pastoral, near Lawrence

Lawrence, in South Otago, was the site of perhaps the most famous and prolific of all New Zealand gold-rush scrambles, at Gabriel's Gully. Newly-arrived fossickers, rooting up tussock clumps on the hills in this vicinity, found sizeable nuggets clinging to the roots. Today, the rolling, green hills carry sheep, and the clang of pick and shovel and the roar of sluices are no longer heard, though it is still possible to pan creeks in the area and win a little colour.

Mount Peel Station and Cabbage Tree ▲

Mount Peel Station is typical of Canterbury back-country sheep runs. The station spreads itself over high hills which are snow-covered during winter, and penetrates far into the foothill ranges up long river valleys. The cabbage tree in the foreground is common in this area and throughout most of pastoral New Zealand. Though having the appearance of a branched palm, it is actually a relation of the lily.

◄ *Four Peaks from Mount Michael, Canterbury*

Reaching up towards the high country, but not so high as to be in tussock or snowgrass country, this back-country station is green and tamed, with orderly wind-breaking shelterbelts and green grasses and clovers abounding.

Arrow Basin ▶

Sheep farming in the Southern Lakes area was begun early in the 1860s, and received an initial boost by having a ready local market in the form of gold-seekers, who flocked to the area in 1863. The climate is one of fairly harsh extremes, which is evident in the arid, rocky aspect of much of the country; but the river valleys, like that of the Arrow River, are fertile and forgiving, and produce good pasture.

hollows and bush in its hanging valleys, and was measured in square miles rather than mere acres. There is mention of blade shearing, with a suspicion of surprise at the time the operation took, and the size of the clip. There is talk of going out and bringing the flock in to sheltered paddocks near the homestead when the weather became rough; and there's a wealth of details of such practices as rubbing rum or brandy on to a ewe's face when persuading her to accept an orphan lamb as her own.

Gradually, the attitudes and practices changed. Gradually the emphasis changed from keeping the new settlements in meat and milk, to selling meat, wool and tallow overseas, mainly to England. Farming became less a matter of subsistence and more a matter of business, and big business, at that.

More and more land was taken up by sheep farmers, and would-be sheep farmers. Dynasties were founded, their fortunes made and assured for years to come, their influence powerful. The farms continued to support the towns, but by the trade they created rather than by the food they supplied.

New Zealand is still very much a sheep country. Cattle are becoming more important, but are still largely raised and fattened as a second string, by sheep men. There are rich dairy areas, notably the Waikato, just to the south of Auckland, and Taranaki, on the West Cape. Dairy farms, until comparatively recently, have been small operations. A small sheep farm, in most areas, would be 280 to 400 hectares. A small dairy farm could be as small as forty hectares; and until perhaps thirty years ago, its produce was consumed by three main markets—cheese factory, butter factory and town milk supply; and even the cheese and butter factories found the greatest market for their produce locally. Today, New Zealand cheese is winning customers in many markets overseas. From a pale yellow cheddar and a slightly orange-coloured process cheese, the range has grown to include blues, smoked cheeses and counterparts of practically every major type of cheese made in Europe or the United States. Butter exports are high, and milk powder, condensed milk and other milk forms and products have won good markets. Dairy farms, therefore, are tending to be larger than they were. Herds have increased since the advent of mechanical milking, and sheds are more sophisticated.

The dairy industry is spread all over New Zealand, (the Waikato and Taranaki being merely the largest areas given over almost entirely to dairying), the main requirement being a good rainfall and country which is not too steep.

High-country sheep stations are generally enormous—hundreds of square kilometres. Many are still huge stations, but on some of them, notably Molesworth in the Marlborough back country, in the heart of the mountains, sheep farming has been abandoned in favour of cattle. Sheep are close grazers and have in the past eaten the heart out of Molesworth. Aerial topdressing and careful pasture rehabilitation and management have transformed the almost desert region into good grazing once more—this time for beef cattle.

Little cereal farming is carried on. The pioneers grew their own wheat and milled it to provide their own flour. The importation of better wheats, notably from Australia, made cereal farming less profitable, and in those flat, alluvial areas where it was once a principal agricultural activity, it has tended to give way to sheep farming. Quite large areas of oats are still sown and harvested, but the golden seas of grain which once clothed the Canterbury Plains, for instance, are gone, and the land is now mostly pasture.

Fields on the Canterbury Plains ▲

The mosaic-like pattern of fields reflects the carving up of squatters' land during the 1880s. Shelter belts protect the mixed crops from the dry nor'-wester.

Mustering, Glen Tanner Station, Mount Cook ▶

The brown, snowgrass-covered country about the feet of the high Alps has an almost desert-like aspect; but it has proved eminently suitable for raising vast flocks of Merino sheep and Merino-based crossbreeds. High, rugged peaks are grazed over in the summer, but the sheep are brought down to the flats for the winter.

Tulip Farm, Waimate ▶

Immigrant Dutch horticulturalists have established themselves in market flower gardens here and there on the Canterbury Plain.

◀ Kerikeri, Northland

It was in this area that the first plough turned the first furrow in New Zealand, in the 1820 s. Agriculture began here, and was well rewarded, for the soil is rich and the climate warm and gentle—one of those blessed places where you 'tickle the earth with a hoe and it laughs a harvest'. Today fruit, especially citrus, is grown here.

Tarawera Farmlands ▼

Typical of the land around the Rotorua area and the great volcanic fault-line, the Tarawera landscape alternated between deep, rift-like, forested valleys and rugged hills, and gentler pasture country, where the grass grows green and lush in the humid climate and rich volcanic soil.

 ◀ *The Ruahine Ranges near Dannevirke*

Pohangina Valley ▶

Typical of central North Island sheep country, this steeply ridged land is seamed with the tracks of sheep along its green faces. Once covered with dense forest, it still protects pockets of bush in its valleys.

Mount Egmont Landscape, Taranaki, North Island ▼

Fairly high annual rainfall and a mild climate combine to make Taranaki farmlands exceptionally rich. Renowned as much for its fine cheeses as its scenes of exquisite pastoral beauty, Taranaki is dominated by Mount Egmont, from whose Maori title the province takes its name.

In the matter of size of sheep farms, Canterbury seems to be the exception which proves the rule. It is, for eighty kilometres north from Ashburton, a place of small farms of forty to eighty hectares. There are exceptions, but the small farms are more common here than anywhere else in the country. They tend to be mixed farms, running sheep, but also producing potatoes, peas, barley, oats and lucerne. From the air, therefore, the plains present a variegated patch-work not seen anywhere else in the country—kilometre after kilometre of green, buff, brown and gold fields, patched by dark pine shelter belts, and divided by vast irrigation races which, tapping the waters of both the rain- and snow-fed rivers, ensure a year-round adequate supply of water.

Canterbury often strikes the visitor as a treeless area. It isn't, as it happens, but there are large areas of flat paddocks, merely patched with what appear to be high, dark hedges, and which are actually shelter brakes of pine, kept neatly trimmed by means of a Heath-Robinson contraption of whirling blades mounted on a tractor. These shelter belts have the important function of breaking the force of the mad nor'wester, a hot sirocco of a wind which romps across the plains with gale force, particularly between September and November.

From Timaru south, the land becomes hilly, and is largely sheep country. It is generally greener here where the land gradually begins to heave itself up towards the foothills of the Alps. It rolls on down to the very edge of the ocean, perching its little townships on river banks.

North Otago hills are equally high, lowering and standing back from the coast around the Waitaki River, and forming a broad, flat plain briefly near Oamaru before becoming humped and high again. This, also, is sheep farming country. In fact, the first shipments of frozen mutton were sent to England from Otago.

Sheep and cattle farming, and some dairying, is the major industry from here south, to Invercargill. In places (such as South Otago's Catlins district), there is a pioneer quality of life, where farms are still being won from heavy forest; but the clearing is no longer haphazard or ill-considered. Farms are often divided by arms of forest, preserved to keep the hills intact and the rich topsoil from being carried down to the rivers.

Cattle are farmed on the narrow coastal strip of Westland, and valiant battles are being fought to prevent some of the fiercer rivers from inundating the farmland, not with water alone, but with gravel and boulders, spoil ripped from the flanks of the mountains by the powerful waters.

To the north, the pattern is not too dissimilar. Northland, which long held the reputation of being a scrubby neck of land, swampy and covered with the pits and scarpings of the hordes of gum diggers who sought the highly-prized *kauri* gum, is really not a bit like that. The almost sub-tropical climate of the Bay of Islands encourages growth. Kerikeri is a fruit-growing centre, mostly citrus fruit, but with apples, tamarillos

and other fruit being produced in quantity. It is a landscape of reddish, tilled earth bordered by intensely green hedges.

Much of the rest of the peninsula is given over to dairy farming, sheep farming on the rolling, central heights, and the country's only remaining *kauri* forests. The *kauri* is a magnificent tree, a sort of antipodean Cedar of Lebanon, with its straight bole, branchless to a considerable height. Great inroads were made into the *kauri* forests of Northland in the nineteenth century, which is understandable, when you look at the trees. They must have made admirable masts and yards for shipping; and the durability of *kauri* timber is legendary. There are trees in those forests

Middlepark Stud, Near Cambridge ▲

Favourably compared with Kentucky Blue Grass country, Cambridge has produced some very fine racehorses and bloodstock.

◀ *Cattle Farming, Karapiro*

Lake Karapiro, in the rich Waikato district, is a man-made lake which was formed by the damming of the Waikato River (part of a hydro-electric scheme). The principal industries hereabouts are beef-cattle and dairy farming, with some stud farming, including the raising and training of racehorses.

which were quite tall youngsters when Jesus walked the earth, and when you cut a good tree down, you cut down two to three thousand years of growth. It takes a long time to replace, which is why the forests are protected today.

There is a seemingly vast forest on the western side of the peninsula, the Waipoua State Forest. But it isn't so vast, really. Some 1 600 hectares of *kauri* and other indigenous trees is a pathetic remnant of the great forests of *kauri* that once covered the land.

The land immediately surrounding Auckland tends to vary from the hummocky swampiness around Helensville to the bush-covered splendour of the Waitakere Ranges. In between those two extremes there is the wine-growing area in the Henderson Valley, heavy, clay soil of which the founder of a local winery said, quoting an old Lebanese proverb: 'The vine shall redeem the waste places of the earth'.

And it has indeed. Some superb wines are produced in this area today.

The Waikato, drained and watered by its great river, and once patched with immense swamps, has always been rich land. Today it is tamed into highly productive dairy land in the south-west, and equally fine sheep country in the north-east. In the days before the Kingite Wars, the Maoris, profiting by the lessons of the missionaries, turned it into their granary. Wheat grew here in prodigious crops. Peaches, almonds, apples, and all manner of vegetables were cultivated. It is still some of the richest soil in New Zealand.

The volcanic plateau for long remained a virtual desert. The acid pumice soil was too poor to support sheep or cattle adequately,

◀ *Kauri Trees, Waipoua State Forest*

After years of unchecked exploitation, the remnants of once-vast *kauri* forests were protected by law. Waipoua State Forest, where these trees are growing, contains several venerable giants in its 16 000 hectares. Perhaps the best known is *Tane Mahuta*, 'God of the Forest', thirteen metres in girth, with its lowest branches some twelve metres from the ground.

and would not grow very much more than the coarse *manuka* scrub that still patches much of it. The radiata pine, however, thrives in it. In the early 1930s, during the depression, relief workers found jobs planting seedlings by hand, and these have grown at a rate unequalled anywhere else in the world. Today, vast forests of pine cover the land with dark green, tossing verdure, and the plateau supports a great forest farming and milling industry, producing timber and paper.

On the east coast of the North Island, Hawkes Bay and the Wairarapa, once heavily timbered, are now gently rolling sheep and cattle country, with the main accent on sheep.

Exotic Forest, Kinleith ▲

In the sour pumice soils of the volcanic plateau, exotic trees, mostly radiata pine, are farmed for pulp and paper manufacture. In an area of man-made forest such as this, as much as 12 000 hectares may be clearfelled each year, and 400 hectares replanted.

Benmore State Hydro-electric Scheme ▲

One of the largest earth dams, and the
largest single power-producing station in
the Southern Hemisphere, Benmore is some
110 metres high and 610 metres long.
Behind it, the Waitaki River has backed up
to form New Zealand's largest man-made
lake, inundating some seventy-seven
square kilometres of high-country farmland.
Trees now grow along stretches of lake
shore, and the effect of the large body of
water on the local climate has been marked.
The brown tussock and desert-like
appearance of much of the lakeside
landscape has given way to green, lush
pasture, uncharacteristic of this part of the
country.

Whakamaru Dam ▶

Whakamaru is one of a series of dams
which make up the vast hydro-electric
scheme on the Waikato River, a 'managed'
river resource from the Lake Taupo to the
Waikato Heads.

It's a crumpled country, with rounded hills and quiet rivers, and three more or less flat stretches—the Heretaunga Plain, dotted with orchards, patched with *raupo* swamps and laced with placid streams; Takapau Plain, narrow, long, slightly humped and edged by the willow-bordered Tukituki River, where sheep and dairy cows graze, and cereal crops are grown; and the wide, flat valley between the Aorangi and Rimutaka Ranges, spreading out as it comes down to Cook Strait, past the broad, shallow waters of Lake Wairarapa and Lake Ferry Lagoon, mostly sheep country, though with some dairying and, around Greytown and Carterton, broad acreages of orchards.

This more-or-less easy, exceedingly fertile pastoral land is separated from the rough, often soggy lowlands south of the Manawatu by country which is not so much crumpled as sharply creased and heavily forested, much of it a wilderness where deer and wild pig roam, (and are hunted), in hidden valleys and alongside bush-shaded river flats.

The 'backblocks' farms reach cleared and grassed fingers deep into this complex of valleys and ridges, and sheep graze paddocks which are still strewn with scatterings of recently cleared bush. Strategic stands of timber hold the hill faces firm against erosion; and, indeed, the worst erosion is still seen to be in the high country east of the ranges, where an earlier generation of frontier farmers cleared incautiously, ignorant of the effects of high rainfall on precipitously steep hillsides deprived of the reinforcing network of great root systems, and the umbrella-like protection of high foliage.

The coastal farms tend to be hummocky, with a water table never far below the surface, and with increasingly broad acreages of sand dunes as the coast sweeps up towards the Wanganui River. It is dairying country, too footwet for sheep. Flax has been grown here, and flaxmills were once common; but improved drainage, while increasing the available grazing land, has done away with the swamps in which *Formium tenax*, the coarse New Zealand flax, used to grow.

Vast areas of New Zealand are set aside as National Parks, where New Zealanders and overseas visitors can enjoy the different types of scenery and wildlife that the country offers. Several million hectares are preserved in this way, the largest being Fiordland National Park, with over one and a quarter million hectares, and the second largest the Urewera National Park, (containing the very lovely Lake Waikaremoana), 2 000 square kilometres of mountainous rainforest country, with deep river valleys and high, misty peaks.

Ferns ▶

◀ *Tarawera Landscape*

New Zealand ferns comprise a wide variety of species, from the great tree ferns such as *Cyathea medullaris* and *Dicksonia squarrosa* to the tiny Filmy Fern, with fronds sometimes only one cell thick. Ferns of this type, *Blechnum discolor*, feature prominently as an element of Maori art, its curved shoots recurring again and again as a carving motif.

◀ *Mountain Daisy*

There are fifty-eight species of Mountain Daisy found in New Zealand, of which these are probably the most familiar. They grow, as the name suggests, in alpine regions, and are large and very showy.

The Kiwi ▲

New Zealand's national emblem, the Kiwi, is a flightless bird, occurring in four main species, three of which are strictly nocturnal. These are the North Island Kiwi, which is the bird most frequently depicted as the country's emblem; the South Island Kiwi, or Tokoeka; the Large Grey Kiwi, or Roa; the Little Grey Kiwi. The Tokoeka which live on Stewart Island are not strictly nocturnal, unlike the others, but may quite often be seen in broad daylight in Stewart Island bush.

Tui on Kowhai Tree ▲

The *tui*, sometimes called the Parson Bird because of the little tuft of white feathers at his throat, is common in forests and reserves throughout New Zealand. About the size of a small raven, with a sheen to his feathers like that of a starling, he is a mimic and a great songster. Most of the singing that falls within the range of the human ear is in the form of clicks, knocking sounds and a bell-like chiming; but his throat can be seen swelling with song too high for the ear to hear.

Kaka Beak ▶

Almost extinct in the wild state, Kaka Beak, (*Clianthus*), was probably saved from extinction by the old-time Maoris, who cultivated it, probably as a source of nectar for caged *tui* birds. The name is derived from the bush parrot, the *kaka*, whose longish, curved bill the flowers resemble. It is seen chiefly as a garden shrub, today.

Mount Cook Lily ▲

Mount Cook Lily, Great Mountain
Buttercup, *Ranunculus lyallii*: three names
to describe a single flower, the best known
of all New Zealand alpine flowers. It is, in
fact, a member of the buttercup family.
New Zealand alpine meadows do not
produce the glorious variety of coloured
blooms which are to be found in a similar
area in Switzerland. They are all white—
but nevertheless, their delicate, waxen
beauty softens an often harsh mountain
landscape.

Kea ▶

The kea, the best-known of New Zealand's
parrots, haunts the snow country of the
South Island.
This cheeky and intelligent bird is
surrounded by controversy as many
runholders believe the kea attacks lambs.

Nature's cauldron – a geothermal wonderland

If you are flying down the east coast of the North Island, over the Bay of Plenty, a little to the south of Tauranga, you'll see White Island, smoking and fuming some kilometres off the mainland shore. And if you look to the starboard side of the aircraft, and the day is fine and clear, you will observe the disturbed land-pattern marking the great volcanic fault-line running through the centre of the North Island, its pathway dotted with extinct, dormant and active volcanoes, steaming lakes, and smoking, steam-wreathed areas of dark scrub and white silica.

It is a weird area, with its warm lakes and its shattered, dead mountains, and it stretches clear from White Island to the central volcanic plateau, pocked and dimpled, with Ruapehu, Tongariro and Ngauruhoe, the three volcanoes, rising up from the wrinkled, seamed earth to the south of Lake Taupo.

At ground level, the netherworldliness of the area is constantly apparent. White Island itself is an uncomfortable place. You reach it by launch from Opotiki, and perhaps wish you hadn't. Here, you keep remembering, men mining sulphur were killed in 1914, in a sudden eruption. You don't wonder at it. You merely wonder what possessed them to stay there at all, for it was then, and is now, a fearsome place, with its snorting fumaroles, its acid lakes and its sulphurous stench.

Sixty to eighty kilometres inland from the mainland coast, a cluster of lakes is set jewel-like in ancient volcanic subsidences— Rotoma, (White or Clear Lake), Rotoehu, (the Bail Lake, or the Lake Shaped like a Canoe Bail), Rotoiti, (Small Lake), and Rotorua, (Lake of the Pit), all fed by cold, rainfed streams which come down through the fissured rock of ancient upheavals, cooled in the shade of the generous rain forest which hides those olden rifts; and they are also fed, here and there, by streams of warm to boiling water, and are occasionally bordered by steaming pools and by whole areas of fumaroles, burbling, slurping, porridge-like boiling mud and spectacular geysers. Farther south, Lake Tarawera spreads over a devastated valley, covering the remains of the once famed Pink and White Terraces, and lapping the shore, at one end of the lake, where the ripped and gashed remains of Mount Tarawera still smoke and tremble. At the other end of the lake, the pathetic remnant of Te Wairoa, once a thriving community and nineteenth century tourist resort, pokes out from the mounded black earth and green grass, known now as Buried Village, and only partially exhumed.

◀ *Steaming Cliffs, Lake Rotomahana*

◀ *Mount Tarawera Volcanic Rent*

On 10 June, 1886, Mount Tarawera
exploded, destroying the Pink and White
Terraces, killing a large number of people,
and burying the village of Te Wairoa. The
highest peak, today, is that in the centre
foreground, 1 498 metres. At the time of
the eruption, the first explosion burst from
the central peak, after which the entire
mountain split in two. The noise of the
volcano was heard as far away as
Coromandel, a distance of a hundred and
sixty kilometres.

Waimangu Valley and Lake Rotomahana ▲

A sightseeing tour, known as the
'Government Round Trip', leads down
through the awesome Waimangu Valley,
site of the great Warbrick Thermal Terrace,
the Waimangu Geyser (which used to be
the world's biggest, playing 450 metres, but
which is now showing signs of its age), and
by launch across Lake Rotomahana, with
its Steaming Cliffs, to Mount Tarawera
and its six kilometre-long gash.

The lakes in this area are rich in certain minerals, which often distinguish them with vivid colours. On the road to Buried Village, for example, the Blue and Green Lakes lie side by side, separated one from the other by a narrow thread of tree-covered land. The names are apt. Blue Lake is a gem of teal blue, regardless of the colour of the sky at the time of viewing. The colour of Green Lake is simply the green of deep water, beautifully translucent.

The same phenomenon is visible in other waters of the area. The infant Waikato River, running away from Lake Taupo, is astonishingly clear and slightly green-tinted, as though it were made of a kind of liquefaction of sunglass-lenses. Its reflecting power seems somewhat diminished, its clarity greatly enhanced, so that you can see the lithe trout which inhabit it, moving and basking in deep pools, plain to see.

Geothermal activity has been harnessed in the Taupo area, at Wairakei. Great lagged pipes run down the valley in stiff, parallel rows, crossing the main road to the power station, where they turn the generator turbines. The steam pressure is considerable, as it must be for the purpose; and you can find a most convincing example of this at the Karapiti Blowhole nearby, whence steam is seen gushing out ceaselessly, at about 1 268 kilopascals pressure, and has been doing so since before there were men on earth. (It is the thermal region's safety valve.) Even so, the project has not been entirely devoid of difficulty. For one thing, the turbines must operate on an absolutely horizontal floor. To ensure this condition in this tremulous area where earth tremors of one magnitude or another are an almost daily occurrence, the power house has had to be flexible, with walls and floors which can move independently of one another.

But above all else, the thermal area is spectacular. There are geysers which spout boiling water to prodigious heights every day, at the same time, regular as clockwork. There are pits of green, boiling water so deep that their bottoms have never been fathomed. There are places where a man, hammering a stake into the ground, has seen it suddenly disappear, its place taken by a whiff of sulphur and a plume of insubstantial steam. There are spas and warm mineral pools where the arthritic come for, and usually find, relief.

The South Island has one or two thermal areas. There is the Maruia Springs resort, on the Lewis Pass road, in a deep valley surrounded by forested mountains and watered by a broad, gravel-bedded river. There is Hanmer, on the eastern side of those same mountains, where hot mineral waters bubble up from the bowels of the earth and are channelled into baths. There are hot springs at the foot of the Franz Josef Glacier, in Westland.

But pride of place goes to the Rotorua area in the North Island, on that great fault line with its mighty chain of steaming lakes and hot pools of bubbling mud.

◀ Mount Ngauruhoe from Ruapehu

The three volcanoes, Ngauruhoe, Tongariro and Ruapehu, smoke and fume high on the North Island's central volcanic plateau. Ngauruhoe is the central peak of the three, a fine symmetrical cone which is actually the offspring of Tongariro, the northernmost volcano, now a shattered series of jagged peaks. Ruapehu, from which this view is obtained, is a truncated cone whose crater contains a steaming lake, the waters of which lap snowy shores around the crater's rim. One of New Zealand's finest skifields is located on Ruapehu.

Mount Ngauruhoe and Lake Taupo ▶

The volcanic origins of the North Island's central plateau are plainly seen in this view of the active volcano, Mount Ngauruhoe, and the nearby gigantic subsidence which forms the bed of Lake Taupo. Here is no slow wrinkling of the earth's crust, but violently-sudden contouring, in geologically-recent times.

Whakarewarewa, Rotorua City and Lake Rotorua ▲

Whakarewarewa, in the foreground, is well named, translating roughly into 'the Valley of Rising Steam'. The area is neatly pathed, and is world famous for its great geysers, its bottomless pools of boiling blue water and its mud and fumaroles. The island on the lake is Mokoia, once the stronghold of the Arawa people. It is also the scene for Maoridom's most famous love story, of Hinemoa and Tutanekai. Tutanekai was a young chief, living on Mokoia Island. Hinemoa was a beautiful maiden living on the mainland shore, and forbidden by her father to see Tutanekai. Tutanekai played his flute one night, and Hinemoa, guided by its music, swam the lake to him.

◄ Warbrick Thermal Terrace, Waimungu

This famous terrace built up of silaceous material layer by layer, is named after a famous Maori guide, Alf Warbrick.

Boiling Mud ▶

Not the least of the fascinations of the thermal areas are the pools of boiling mud. The constantly changing patterns and the colours which vary from chocolate brown to slate grey provide great photographic opportunity; and the activity is sufficiently sluggish to allow a closer approach than is possible with geysers and hot water or steam activities.

◀ *Geothermal Activity, Whakarewarewa*

Pohutu Geyser, Whakarewarewa ▶

One of the most spectacular of the area's geysers, Pohutu plays frequently, hurling steam-plumed jets of boiling water high into the air.

Opposite page:
Mount Ngauruhoe, Tongariro National Park

There is more or less constant activity from Mount Ngauruhoe's crater. Mostly taking the form of a plume of steam, it can erupt with startling vigour and little warning, sending great, billowing clouds of smoke into the sky and powdering the snowfields with ash. Usually, however, some warning is given by its gradually increasing activity.

Bottom: Orakei Korako

Orakei Korako, thirty-odd kilometres north of Taupo, steadily declined as a thermal attraction, its activity diminishing at a rapid rate until, in 1961, a hydro-electric dam across the Waikato River caused the water to back up and form Lake Ohakuri. Immediately, Orakei Korako burst into new life. Principal attractions are Hochstetter Cauldron, ejecting four and a half million litres of boiling water per day; Lady Cobham Geyser; Rainbow Terrace; and the fabulous Golden Fleece.

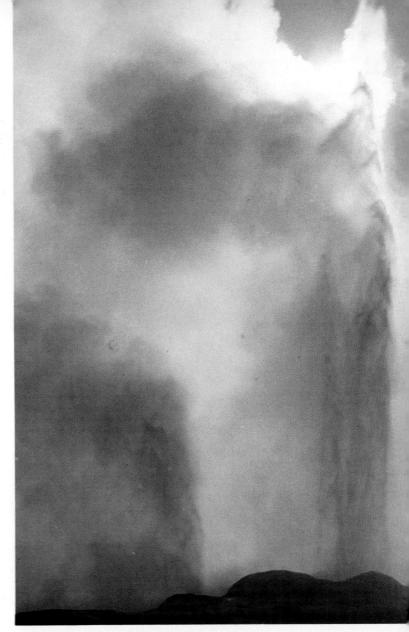

Tongariro National Park and Mount Ngauruhoe

Tongariro National Park was originally presented to the nation by the Chief, Te Heu Heu Tukino. It offers recreational facilities for skiers, trampers, climbers and people who enjoy exploring bush walks and areas of thermal activity.

112

First published 1975
Reprinted 1976
Revised edition 1977
Reprinted 1978, 1979, 1980, 1981, 1982, 1984, 1985
1987
by Golden Press Pty Ltd
16 Copsey Place
Avondale, Auckland
Printed in Hong Kong
ISBN 0 85558 4 327
© Robin Smith and W. Warren Jacobs

We are indebted to Mount Cook Airlines
for their generous assistance in air travel,
and to the people throughout the country
who freely assisted us in many ways

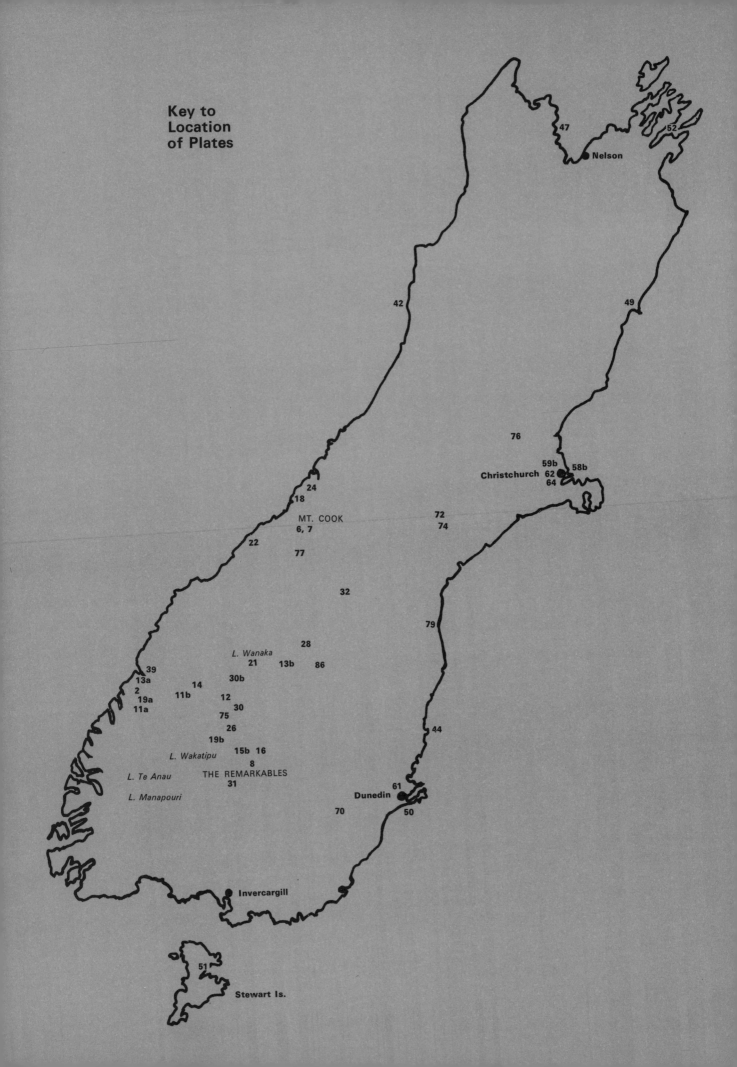

Key to
Location
of Plates